Learning Technology

# Learning Technology

Gordon Lewis

OXFORD
UNIVERSITY PRESS

Great Clarendon Street, Oxford, OX2 6DP, United Kingdom

Oxford University Press is a department of the University of Oxford.
It furthers the University's objective of excellence in research, scholarship,
and education by publishing worldwide. Oxford is a registered trade
mark of Oxford University Press in the UK and in certain other countries

ISBN: 978 0 19 420041 7

Printed in China

This book is printed on paper from certified and well-managed sources

ACKNOWLEDGEMENTS

*Back cover photograph*: Oxford University Press building/David Fisher.

*The publisher is grateful to those who have given permission to reproduce the following
photographs and screenshots*: p.22 tpack.org © 2012. p.47 © Mike Harrison
(www.mikejharrison.com). p.49 Nicholas Lewis (Mountains). p.56 Shaun
Wilden (Trainer). p.61 Gordon Lewis (Landscapes, Windsurfer, Sign, Yacht).
p.65 *Together* (VLE Menu) Oxford University Press. p.69 *English File* (Test Builder)
Oxford University Press. p.71 *Mosaic* (Gradebook) Oxford University Press.
p.94 *Together* (Language Game) Oxford University Press.

*Screenshots from the following websites are used which feature search terms or content
generated by the author*: p.31 www.diigo.com. p.32 www.feedreader.com.
pp.38–39 www.surveymonkey.com. p.40 www.google.com/edu.
p.49 www.wikispaces.com. p.53 Apple iTunes. p.56 www.youtube.com.
p.61 www.flickr.com. p.66 www.edmodo.com. p.69 www.easytestmaker.com.
p.73 www.socrative.com. p.93 www.duolingo.com.

# Acknowledgements

Writing about technology is like shooting at a constantly moving target, and I am grateful to many people for providing encouragement, inspiration, and focus in the process of creating this book.

I'd like to thank the team at Laureate Education, especially Joseline Castaños, Christopher Johnson, Shannon Olson, Arnoldo Lezama, Cinthya Marisol Gonzalez Maldonado, and Ana Gabriela Morazán Salgado, for having my back when the writing got intense. I also want to highlight the great efforts of the Laureate Languages teams around the world in making blended language learning a success at their institutions. Their experiences, ideas, and suggestions were pivotal in writing this book. A special shout out to Danny Lowe in Honduras who demonstrates best practice in technology integration every day.

In addition to my colleagues at Laureate, I also want to thank the Hopewell Valley Regional School District, NJ, for their great efforts at building a district-wide technology plan. Special thanks to my partner on the technology committee, Tony Suozzo, and of course the superintendent, Tom Smith, who provided access to the schools to observe learning technology in action.

A huge thanks to Julia Bell, Helen Wendholt, Andrew Dilger, Danielle King, and Duncan Laing at Oxford University Press for being so patient with me in getting this book completed. As always, their insights and editorial support make me a better writer.

Finally, thanks to my wife, Katja, who gave up family time so this project could be completed on time. And to the dogs, Lucy and Sammy, and Charlotte the cat, for keeping me company.

# Contents

# Introduction

## The challenge of learning technology

Learning technology is not new. Almost as long as there have been teachers, there have been instructional tools to help students learn, from clay slates, the abacus, pencils and pens, typewriters, overhead projectors, and computers, to the internet, smartphones, and **social networks**. There has been an ever-accelerating cycle of innovation in the development of teaching tools, yet the classroom challenges have remained essentially the same: how do we 'reach' our students? How can we challenge and motivate them to think for themselves? How can we use the tools at our disposal to improve the classroom experience?

There is little doubt that new learning technologies open up possibilities beyond reach in previous eras. However, such technologies will have only limited impact if the pedagogy behind their application does not keep pace. Technology is nothing without a teacher and a plan.

It is probably safe to say that most educated people will have little difficulty understanding the basics of technology; the real knowledge gap lies in its application. There is still a huge divide between the teaching strategies of the analogue classroom and the digital world in which we live.

This book aims to bridge this divide by identifying the potential ways in which learning technology can be used to facilitate and enhance current classroom practice. Additional material can be found on the website accompanying the book (www.oup.com/elt/teacher/itc). Together, the book and the website materials provide a solid framework for technology integration and practical examples of activities to help you, the teacher, feel confident in making educated choices on introducing and implementing learning technology in your classroom.

## 21st century skills

It is almost impossible to predict what the future will hold more than a few years ahead. Some people have predicted that 80% of all future jobs have not even been created yet. This has huge implications for education and society as a whole. How can we prepare the next generation of students for the increasingly competitive global marketplace if we do not even know what this marketplace is going to look like? Without a doubt, technology is driving these changes, and being a competent user of technology is a key 21st century skill. For this reason alone, we need to integrate technology into our learning and teaching.

## Focusing on language

Many of your students will be interested in using technology because it is new and exciting. Although it is good to encourage this interest, you also need to bear in mind your language teaching goals. As you consider implementing technology in the classroom, always have your ultimate language learning goals clearly in focus. It is very easy for students to get carried away and spend valuable language learning time creating colourful graphics or embedding animations in slide shows which contribute next to nothing to the language learning process. This is not to say that we should discourage students from using technology creatively. It can be a great motivator and help increase students' pride in their work. However, there needs to be a clearly defined language focus in each activity for it to be meaningful.

A note on terminology: with the growth of smartphones, tablets, and **cloud computing**, the same content and functionality can be accessed from multiple machines. For this reason, we will use the broader term 'device' instead of the individual terms where appropriate.

## A word of reassurance

In today's world, it would be inappropriate to try and teach through the printed word alone. Using technology is no longer a choice; it is a necessity. But don't let yourself feel intimidated by new technology. Don't let new words and phrases like **adaptive learning** or cloud computing confuse you. The rapid pace of new developments means that almost everyone is adjusting and learning as they go along. There is no right or wrong way of integrating learning technology, and you don't need to follow the latest trend just because anyone else is. Basic technologies can, in many cases, achieve the same or similar results as using more sophisticated **apps**. Don't worry about being completely up to date; new technology is introduced every day. Just use what works for you.

## How this book is organized

In Part 1, we will look at broad issues of technology planning and how we can develop strategies for technology integration. We will pay particular attention to training and professional development. In Part 2, we will turn our attention to popular technology tools found in classrooms today and provide examples of how they can be effectively used in language teaching. In Part 3, we look beyond individual tools to explore systems and educational approaches which are transforming the way we teach and learn. Finally, in Part 4, we take a peek into the future and consider what is on the horizon for educational technology.

Although there are many links between the chapters in the book, you do not need to read them in order. Each chapter can be read on its own, and the ideas presented will give you tools and techniques that can be used with students covering various teaching areas.

The main text of the book deals with the pedagogy behind each topic discussed in connection with learning technology. *Try this* activities provide specific ideas and techniques that you can try immediately. *Getting it right* sections give procedural tips for some of the more specific suggestions. *Why this works* sections provide pedagogic rationale for activities where it is important and helpful to do so. In addition, the Glossary provides explanatory notes on words that appear in bold throughout the main text, and the *Useful websites* section lists online resources for extending or developing activities discussed in the book.

# Part 1        Developing a technology plan

# 1     Define your teaching model

## From learning technology to digital learning

Learning technology has been around for centuries, but what has changed over the past generation or so is the pace of innovation. The sheer vastness of learning technology in an ever-developing field of language education brings about countless opportunities for teachers and students, but it also has the potential to overwhelm them and create anxiety and resistance. The need for support and careful, measured introduction of new tools and resources is a prerequisite for their successful adoption. Good planning is key.

## Identifying your personal technology profile

This is the first step in the adoption process – assessing your own readiness to embrace new technology.

Technology experts frequently use the terms 'digital natives' versus 'digital immigrants'. Basically, a digital native is someone who has grown up with digital technology, whereas a digital immigrant is someone who grew up without digital technology and adopted it as an adult.

The majority of students and teachers are probably digital natives, but this does not mean that the social use of technology has crossed over to the language classroom. There is still a need for many teachers to assimilate into the world of digital education. Read the three descriptions below and decide which best describes you.

1 **Casual user:** You use technology in your daily teaching life. You are comfortable searching the internet for information. Although you may have access to technology in your classroom, you only occasionally use it; and when you do, it is likely to be supplemental and not integrated into your lesson plans.
2 **Old schooler:** You have adopted technology in your daily teaching life, but you use it in much the same way you use more traditional classroom tools. You may create worksheets and handouts for your students, or get them to use software programs, to practise and support what they have learnt. Technology plays a complementary role in your established lesson plans. It supports and may even extend learning, but it does not fundamentally change the way you teach.
3 **Innovator:** You embrace technology in ways that not only support the learning process, but also transform it. You use technology to promote learner autonomy and support critical and creative thinking and problem-solving skills. You infuse your lessons with real-life content,

promote authentic communication, and provide opportunities for students to produce language through a variety of different media, sharing what they make with a range of audiences, both local and global.

## Adoption cycle

Over the past decade, researchers have identified certain behaviours when introducing new learning technologies into schools and other educational institutions. These behaviours have been mapped out onto what is known as the adoption cycle (see Figure 1.1). The size of each category reflects the percentage of adopters at each phase. Thinking in terms of individual technology profiles, where do you think you and your colleagues would line up on this curve? What percentage of your teaching staff (or students, for that matter) would fall into each category?

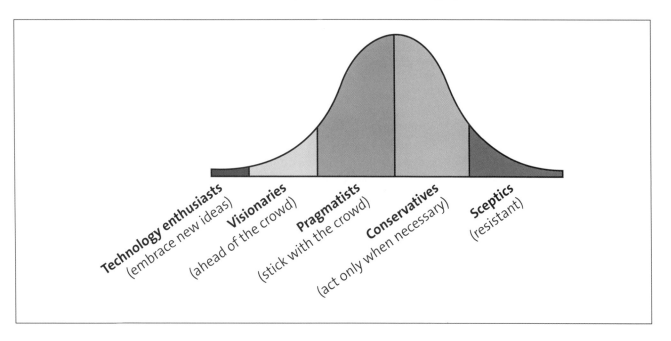

FIGURE 1.1    *Adoption cycle (based on the Technology Adoption Life Cycle)*

Adoptions of technology go through phases in much the same way as in the adoption cycle described above. Another way of looking at technology adoption, however, is to focus on the technology tool itself. Figure 1.2 illustrates the life cycle of a particular technology.

As Figure 1.2 demonstrates, the first reaction to new learning technologies is generally very enthusiastic. In fact, the reaction to something new is often 'over-heated'. However, after this initial enthusiasm and once teachers actually take the time to try out the tool, they can become frustrated, perhaps not understanding how to really use it. Taking the time to understand the tool can be time-consuming and complicated, leading to a strong dip in confidence as users realize that technology is only as good as the ideas that drive its application.

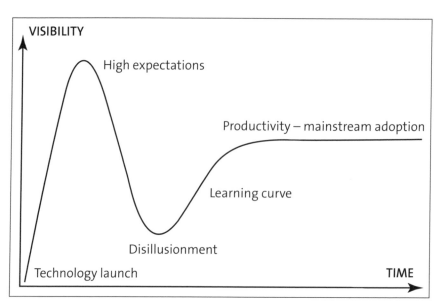

FIGURE I.2    *Technology life cycle (based on the Gartner Hype Cycle)*

Slowly, over time, this negative reaction gives way to a more pragmatic approach to the new learning technology, which ends in a productive use of it in the teaching process. How smoothly this transition takes place is dependent on effective training and support. A strong professional development plan can eliminate the highs and lows of the technology life cycle and flatten your own learning curve.

What is interesting to consider is the relationship between Figures 1.1 and 1.2. Technology enthusiasts and visionaries enthusiastically embrace new technologies, but they struggle to persuade pragmatists to share their enthusiasm. This is known as the 'chasm' – the gap between the 'converted' and the majority who may be nervous and fearful of change. It is a gap that is difficult to bridge. Any good learning technology plan needs to acknowledge this, and find a way to lead the majority to a successful adoption of the technology.

**Try this** ☞    **Adoption cycle**

Think about any changes that have taken place in your current workplace. They need not be technology related; it could be a new way of evaluating teachers or the introduction of a new schedule. How did you and your colleagues adjust? Using the adoption cycle (see Figure 1.1), place yourself and your colleagues in the appropriate categories. Do you think you would be in the same category with regard to technology innovation?

 **Getting it right**

## Creating an individual technology plan

In order to most effectively harness the power of technology, whether at the individual classroom level or at the level of an institution as whole, there are some key questions to bear in mind.

### 1 What are the concrete advantages?

Look at each element of technology you intend to use and try to define its specific value to your teaching and your students' learning. Will the technology facilitate collaboration? Will it make your job as a teacher easier by making planning more efficient? Will using it make learning more authentic and relevant to learners? Thinking hard about these questions in advance will go a long way to helping you decide if your technology is a fun add-on or an integrated tool.

### 2 How does technology fit in with the existing system – its norms, values, and goals?

Think about how you teach and the way you want your students to learn. There is no one right way to learn, and the technology you choose should reflect your beliefs and be appropriate for the educational context in which you work.

### 3 How hard is it to use?

Not all technology implementation is worth the immediate effort. Although technology integration may have a positive mid- to long-term impact on teaching and learning, you need to weigh this against your larger priorities and, perhaps, choose to wait before diving into something complex which could distract you and your students from these priorities. Even if you feel confident with a tool, you certainly don't want to spend a great deal of classroom time helping students understand how to use it.

### 4 Is it visible?

How significant a role will the technology play in your teaching? Will the tool overpower the task? What is the risk of distraction? Many educators argue that the best implementations of technology are those where the technology blends into the background and becomes invisible in the teaching process.

*5 Can you measure it?*

Although technology should not drive the lesson, we do need to find ways to measure its impact. It can be helpful to ask yourself three very simple questions and to think of examples for the answer to each.

1 Did my students like the new technology?
2 Did they learn using the new technology?
3 Are they using the new technology to demonstrate what they have learnt?

---

**Try this**     **Matching technology and pedagogy: lesson planning**

Think about a typical lesson you teach. What activities do you use? Do you include group and project work, or ask students to make oral presentations? Write down the most frequent activity types that you employ and match the activities to a list of technology tools, such as presentation software, **wikis**, **blogs**, or smartphone cameras. Try out the selected tool. Do you think using the tool improves the activity?

## Institutional technology plans

Unless you are self-employed or a freelance teacher/trainer, your use of technology will take place in the context of a learning organization, be it a school, a university, or a corporate training entity. As you develop your own strategies for using learning technology, you will want to align them to your institution's strategic vision and teaching guidelines – often captured in an institutional technology plan. Will this plan support what you want to do? Think about the following two areas of support.

1 **Technical support:** Technology doesn't always work. Do you have a technology support team to fix problems that arise with hardware and software? Maybe you just want to learn how to use a piece of software. Is there a person to contact for training? There should be a clear process in place for dealing with technology issues, preferably with a tracking system to trace the steps in solving the problem. In some cases, your technology support team will not be able to solve a problem and will have to submit the problem to an external provider – for example, if you are using a virtual learning environment (see Chapter 7).

2 **Administrative support:** What happens if you want to purchase new technology for your classroom? Who organizes the purchase? Is there a process in place to do this? How do you manage shared resources? Is someone responsible for scheduling access to technology? If you have access to a computer lab or share a set of tablets, is someone responsible for maintaining the calendar?

**✓ *Getting it right***    **Identifying your personal technology profile**

Developing a technology plan is not a one-off activity or something that is done once every five years. Each technology plan should be developed for a 3- to 5-year period but reviewed and updated annually. In other words, a 2017–2020 plan should be reviewed in 2018 and become the 2018–2021 plan, and so on, depending on the duration of the plan in action. In this way, your plan will always be current and aligned to the vision of your institution.

## Assessing the impact of technology

It is notoriously difficult to accurately measure the impact of technology on student success. Unless you are able to compare a control group that does not use technology to your technology-infused classes, it will be hard to definitively prove technology's impact on learning outcomes. Therefore, it is important to set your expectations as concretely as possible. What are these expectations? For instance, specific improvements in learning outcomes as measured in terms of language proficiency? Increased self- and student motivation? Or for technology to make your life easier as a teacher by making lesson planning, assessment, and content creation more efficient?

## Getting started

### What you need to get started

The essentials you need in order to introduce technology to your classroom are outlined below.

1 **A computer with internet connection:** Generally speaking, your computer should have at least 4 GB of RAM and a built-in **hard drive** with a minimum of 250 GB of storage, if possible. High-speed internet connection, known as **broadband**, can be accessed wirelessly and via fibre-optic cable, modems, and mobile phone networks.
2 **A printer:** If possible, print work in colour for final projects or display purposes and in black and white for working copies.

The following types of hardware can also be useful and motivating tools.

1 **A webcam:** If you want to conduct whole-class webcam activities, it is worth investing in a quality webcam with a resolution high enough to provide a clear picture on a large screen.
2 **A camera:** Unless you are a serious photographer and want to photograph in difficult conditions, smartphones should have everything you need to take great photos.
3 **A scanner:** This is particularly useful if you want to create a record of student work such as an e-portfolio. You can work offline and store the results electronically.
4 **A video camera:** Digital video cameras are really only necessary for creating professional videos with effects requiring complex editing. Otherwise, the video recording function on smartphones is adequate.

# 2    Being aware of the issues

## Browsing safely

The internet can be a dangerous place if you don't pay attention to security. Dangers can range from relatively benign spam (unwanted email) to **viruses** which can cause you to lose all your data. Perhaps more ominous, the anonymous nature of the **world wide web** ('web' for short) allows unscrupulous people to steal your information, or even your identity. For unsuspecting young internet users, it allows them to establish friendships with people on the web without ever meeting them face-to-face, only to find out later that a 'friend' is a predator. Clearly, internet security needs to be taken very seriously.

## The six golden rules of internet security

### 1 Never share personal information online

The ability to communicate across the world opens up amazing opportunities, but it can also be risky. You can never be one hundred per cent sure who you are talking to when you contact people on the web. In order to protect yourself and your students, never reveal any personal information such as addresses or telephone numbers, and be especially careful about posting photographs on a website. If you conduct class projects with a partner school, check that the information is protected. With school-age children, be sure to get written consent from a parent/carer for a student's picture to appear on a website. Failure to do so can lead to lawsuits against you and your institution.

### 2 Install antivirus software

A virus is a covert program or piece of code that can potentially harm, or even destroy, your data. There are many different types of viruses, such as spyware (which tracks your movements on the web) and malware (which damages your software). There are a number of antivirus programs available on the web which update automatically when you access the internet. While these programs try and keep up with threats, there is no perfect protection, so if you don't recognize a link or an email, think twice before you click on it.

### 3 Enable the firewall on your computer

A **firewall** blocks access to your computer from unapproved users and websites. Today, it is quite common for people to try to 'hack' into computer systems to gain unauthorized access to their files and programs. The hacker may do this for fun or with the aim of stealing or deleting your data. In some cases, hackers infiltrate a computer to commit a crime, such as taking a user's personal details to commit fraud.

Most modern **operating systems** have built-in firewalls. Ensure that they are turned on before you go online. You can do this on a Windows-based operating system by opening up the control panel and clicking on the Windows firewall icon. Here you can set the level of protection you require, making exceptions for websites you trust and use frequently.

### 4 Do not open email attachments from unfamiliar addresses

Many viruses use email attachments to gain access to your computer. When you open the attachment, the virus is released. Be wary of any email from an unknown sender, especially if the sender has addressed you in a very personal way or has tried to gain your interest by adding a personal subject header. Be sure to screen the email with your antivirus software. Even if you know the sender, you should screen all emails, as the sender may not be aware that their email is infected. In some cases, a hacker can get into someone's address book and infiltrate their email account, sending illicit emails from their address.

### 5 Always log off

The more time you spend unnecessarily connected, the greater the likelihood you may be attacked. Instead of leaving an app running in the background while you do something else, be sure to disconnect.

### 6 Always back up your data

Nothing is more frustrating than having a computer crash and lose all your data. Play it safe and back up your data regularly – at least once a week.

## Copyright and plagiarism

The same copyright law applies to material on the web as it does to books, magazines, and other published material. However, because information is so easy to access on the internet, many students (and teachers) consider copying content from the internet a trivial offence – somehow different from taking passages from a book. It is as if online material somehow belongs to everybody the moment it is added to the web.

One reason for this is the ease with which one can copy, paste, or **download** text, images, and audio/video files from the web. There are, however, four very clear guidelines on copyright which you should discuss with your students and follow yourself.

1   It is fine to **hyperlink**. You can connect your website to another acceptable website on the web (obviously not websites displaying inappropriate material).

2   Do not take information from a website unless permission is given by the author(s). This permission is often stated on the website, but in cases where it is not, you should write to the webmaster/author of the website

in question and make a formal written request to use the material. Many websites allow use for educational purposes but restrict commercial use.

3  It is permissible to use copyrighted material for a purpose beyond and/or different from the author's original intention. In other words, using a segment from a film (for example, a trailer) to create a film review would be acceptable use of the copyrighted material ('fair use'). Fair use can also be measured in terms of the amount of material used. Copying an entire text is much less likely to be considered fair than copying a short paragraph. This consideration has a lot to do with the financial impact of the use in question. Obviously, if you download a copyrighted text in its entirety, you are taking away from the author's potential market for the material. Fair use is interpreted differently from country to country, so check your local laws.

4  You are on safest ground with material which is open to everybody, i.e. work that is not protected by copyright and belongs in what we call the 'public domain'. Many authors and organizations post their material to the public domain from the start. Other material enters the public domain when its copyright expires. Most websites will explicitly state whether their material is copyrighted. However, when in doubt it is always a good idea to assume that the content is protected. If you wish to use this content, contact the website owners. They may have no objection if it is to be used for educational purposes.

There are also organizations which manage public domain material. A good place to start is Creative Commons, which awards licences to authors interested in sharing their work with others without complicated copyright restrictions (See *Useful websites*). There are various levels of licences. Some licences allow for sharing but forbid commercial use of the materials. Others allow sharing but not modification of the material. You can search the website for text, images, and audio/video files, as well as the type of licence that fits your needs.

Two other websites with public domain material which are useful in language teaching are the Internet Archive and Project Gutenberg (See *Useful websites*). The former archives films, text, audio, software, and digital educational resources. It also has excellent hyperlinks to many other websites. Project Gutenberg is the largest collection of free e-books in the world.

 *Getting it right*

**How to identify plagiarized passages**

Some students are very bold about plagiarizing – that is, copying – whole sections of text and pasting it into their own work. If you are in any doubt about a segment of text in a student's work, highlight a small section and paste it into a **search engine**. The search often reveals the passage the material was taken from.

# Training and professional development

Let's assume you have all the technology you want at your disposal. Now you and your colleagues have to learn how to use it. Training is the big hidden cost in technology implementation. Below are some tips to make training popular and effective.

- **Training should be regular and consistent.** Develop a training plan for the entire year and stick to it. Like students, teachers want predictability.
- **Training should be delivered in small doses.** Technology training does not lend itself to intensive delivery. If you do a one-week intensive pre-service seminar, you can be sure that much of what is learnt will not be retained. Also, teachers are busy people who need to prepare classes, grade student work, and so on. Consider keeping training sessions to under an hour, but hold them frequently.
- **Focus on one key point per session.** Do not try to cover too much ground in each session. Introduce one tool or app at a time.
- **Encourage peer teaching.** Rather than teaching technology skills from the top down, have teachers teach each other. This will build teacher confidence and promote community building and resource sharing. Look for technology champions among your staff who would be willing to serve as trainers.
- **Teach skills that teachers can take away and use.** Make sure the skills you teach in each session are practical and relevant to activities they can use in their classrooms with a minimum of modification.
- **Work with the learning technology companies.** If your school has recently bought new technology, get the local company to provide training to your teachers. They should be willing to do this for free or at a minimal cost. They can talk your staff through the more technical aspects of the tools and you can focus on their educational use.
- **Try it out yourself first.** Before you introduce any technology-based activities into the classroom, try out the technology tools yourself. Correct a document with track changes, make a PowerPoint presentation, blog, or wiki. Experiment with adding pictures, or even video and audio to a document. Practice makes perfect. Once you feel confident using a tool, you will be better able to guide your students.

## TPACK model

The technological pedagogical content knowledge (TPACK) model is very useful in defining professional development for learning technology integration. TPACK identifies three distinct domains of knowledge and skills that a teacher must master to effectively integrate technology.

1 **Technical knowledge:** In order to use technology effectively, you have to know how it works. This is the practical knowledge of a tool and its functions. You can't drive a car if you can't turn on the engine, put the car in gear, etc. If you don't master the basic functionality of a specific technology, you will be distracted and uncertain in your classroom.
2 **Content knowledge:** This refers to the depth of knowledge a teacher has in the specific subject he or she is teaching.

3  **Pedagogical knowledge:** Even though you may know a lot about a subject, if you don't have the skills to transmit that knowledge to your students, you will not be an effective teacher. While most teaching best practices can apply to teaching with technology, there are additional pedagogical elements to be considered, such as pacing in online environments, giving feedback online or creating and assessing multimedia content. These new elements should not be seen as add-ons to teacher education but should be part of the core of any good teacher training programme.

As Figure 2.1 shows, in order to be an effective teacher in the 21st century, you should have competence in all three knowledge domains.

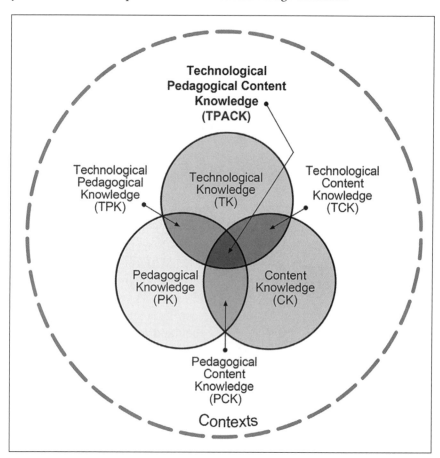

FIGURE 2.1     *TPACK training model*

**Try this** 👉  **Create a TPACK diagram**

Create a blank TPACK diagram such as the one in Figure 2.1. Choose a learning point you teach regularly and put it into the 'content knowledge' circle. Next, choose a teaching strategy or activity you would use to teach this point to your students. Put the strategy in the 'pedagogical knowledge' circle. Finally, choose a technology tool to deliver the lesson content and put that in the 'technological knowledge' circle. Do the three elements harmonize? What adjustments could you make?

## Personal learning networks and communities of practice

Today's teachers need to be lifelong learners, but many teacher training and development programmes remain stuck in the 20th-century models. These old models are predominantly linear, as opposed to integrated like the TPACK model, with a focus on training and not development. While linear training models will continue to have a legitimate place in teacher education, opportunities for peer-to-peer collaboration and mentorship are extending this learning, providing opportunities for teachers to learn what they need to know, when they need to know it, from colleagues around the world or next door.

**Personal learning networks (PLNs)** unite teachers around the world. Unlike established groups that you can join online, you create your own PLN and link it to resources based on your specific needs and interests. PLNs are personal. **Communities of practice**, on the other hand, are not based on the individual. They consist of people working together towards a common goal, exchanging ideas to find innovative solutions to challenges in their shared domain. This idea is based on a mentorship model, but social networking technologies make it possible to communicate across physical boundaries and capture best practice to make it accessible across an entire **network**. As a teacher, you can manage your own PLN and also be deeply involved in any number of communities.

 *Getting it right*

**Personal learning networks**

Since a PLN is personal, you need to feel comfortable with the tools you choose to use. Ask yourself: how do you like to communicate: via a blog, email, Twitter, Facebook, or LinkedIn? Do you want to talk to people in real time via **videoconference** or **instant messaging**? Who do you want to communicate with? Are there specific groups you would like to link to? Will you join other communities? How do you want to manage information you may receive or share? Once you have established a PLN that fits your needs, you can ask a question to your network. Be aware that if an answer is not forthcoming, you may still need to look for a document or resource that can answer your question, or get training that will help you acquire the skills to answer the question yourself.

# Part 2    Using online tools

# 3

# The web and the cloud

## What exactly is the world wide web?

Have you ever stopped to ask yourself what the world wide web is? To most people, the world wide web and the internet are synonymous, but this is not the case. The internet is a huge network of connected computers, linked across the world. For example, email is on the internet but is not part of the world wide web. The world wide web, however, is the part of the internet where information can be accessed. It's the colourful, fun part of the internet, consisting of a limitless and ever-expanding number of pages which we navigate using **web browser (browser)**. It is a means of communicating rather than accessing information. Besides being fun, what are the advantages of using the world wide web in our classrooms? Below are a few advantages that come to mind.

- **The web provides authentic content.** Students and teachers get limitless, 'real' content in the target language. They can read a real menu, find out what time a train departs, listen to a sports broadcast, or watch a film trailer. The web can enrich your coursebook by bringing language learning to life. Let's not forget that the web can also provide you with lesson plans, ideas banks, test generators, and pretty much anything else you would want to utilize as a teacher.
- **The web offers meaningful language.** Studies have shown that students learn language better when the language they are exposed to is meaningful. The web creates contexts for language use which, through their authenticity, become purposeful in the eyes of the students. The students actively manipulate the language for a clear and logical purpose.
- **The web promotes critical thinking skills and 'constructivist' learning.** On the web, knowledge is transient. Unlike coursebooks, which transmit information in a predictable order, the web is constantly evolving. Students make choices and 'construct' knowledge every time they go online. Each search is unique.
- **The web reduces focus on the teacher.** Working with the web can take the focus off you and shift communication from being teacher–student to being student–student. If you are a bit unsure of your own English language skills, authentic listening and reading materials from the web can help model the language you want to teach.
- **Web-based work can increase motivation.** The web is colourful, exciting, and undeniably 'cool'. Computers, mobile devices, and the web are key components of youth culture and can lend credibility to language learning when used in the classroom.

## Searching online

### Web browsers

Web browsers are your door to the web. Essentially, browsers read the html code that they receive from a website. This code tells the browser how to display information on your computer. Think of a browser as a little TV that gets signals from a broadcasting station. Like a TV, each browser reads the 'signal' slightly differently, so websites may not always appear exactly the same.

In the early days of the web, most information was either text or simple images (photographs or drawings). However, today the web is full of multimedia: audio files, video, and animation formats. Not all browsers have the software to display every format. When a browser comes across a format it can't display, it automatically looks for a program called a **plug-in**. If you have the required plug-in on your computer, it will automatically display the requested content. If the plug-in isn't already installed on your computer, you will need to download it from the web. Typical plug-ins you should be sure to have installed on your computer are outlined below.

- Media players (such as RealPlayer, Windows Media Player, or QuickTime): Media players allow you to play video and audio files.
- Adobe Acrobat: This allows you to display documents formatted as **PDFs** (files which can be read without a word processing program).
- HTML5 and Shockwave Flash: These allow you to open web animation files. HTML5 is a new type of code (that is quickly replacing Shockwave Flash) which allows for responsive design. This gives the websites the ability to adjust to the device they are being displayed on, such as computers, tablets, and smartphones.
- Java: This is a type of programming language which sends instructions to a computer. It can be used across multiple computer platforms, making it very practical for the internet. Applets (mini-programs that run in Java) can be used on websites to make the page fun and interactive.

Choosing a browser is a matter of personal preference. For example, Google Chrome would be an obvious choice for those using other Google apps. However, while there are differences between browsers, any of the popular options should provide all the functionality you need for normal computing needs.

 *Getting it right*

**Bugs in software**

Be aware that the very latest version of any software may contain 'bugs' – errors in programming code – which are only discovered once they are released. Before installing the latest version, search online to see if any other users have come across a bug. If there is a bug, the software company will usually release a 'patch' – a smaller piece of software designed to update the previous release – to fix the problem, so make sure you download the patch as soon as it becomes available.

## Search engines

If a browser is your gateway to the web, a search engine is your guide to its contents. Certainly, if you were to know the **web address** of each website you wanted to visit, there would be no need for you to use a search engine. However, this is like saying you know exactly which books you want to look for in a library and where to find them. As the web is a library of over one billion websites (and rising), this is unlikely.

In order to help people find their way around the web, programmers created search engines – websites that allow you to search the web by typing in **keywords** and queries. The most well known of these search engines is undoubtedly Google. In fact, Google is so common in today's world that 'to google' has become a common verb in English and many other languages. However, Google isn't the only search engine available. There are many other options (e.g. Yahoo! and Bing), including search engines geared towards specific types of content, such as children's websites, business websites, people-searching websites, job websites, and, of course, websites defined by language or geography. You may also find that some websites have a search engine **widget**, so you can search directly from the website. A search engine takes into account a variety of factors. It will search for the keywords you type, calculate the relevance of the website, and rank the search results by popularity. How you search will largely be dependent on your own knowledge and understanding of how information is linked. The search engine tries to interpret your intentions and deliver a set of results based on this logic. Sometimes the results yield immediate benefits, but more often than not, the results will need to be refined.

 *Getting it right*

### Web directories

As well as search engines, there are also web directories which are actually very different. On web directories, websites are organised into categories. If you know what you are looking for, web directories can save time, much like looking through a telephone book.

Not all information on a website will be captured by the search engine, which may result in follow-up searches. For example, you may decide to visit the first website on the list of search engine results which, in turn, has hyperlinks to other websites. You may follow one of these hyperlinks, and soon you will find yourself very far away from the search engine results page you first started with. Thankfully, your browser has a very useful function called 'history', which lists all of the websites you have visited by date and time; so if you find yourself completely lost, you will be able to retrace your steps. (Each browser has a slightly different way to access search histories. On Microsoft Edge, for example, you have to click on the clock icon in the 'hub' menu. On Firefox, your history can be found by clicking on the three horizontal lines icon on the top right corner of your screen.)

**Try this** ☞ **Searching the web**

Assign your students a search activity to perform in class. Give them 15 minutes to research a topic or a set of questions. Ask the students to share their search histories with the class. Discuss how different students approached the task. Did some search quickly through many websites? How deep into each website did they go? Discuss whether certain ways of searching were more effective than others.

 *Getting it right*

**How to search the web**

There is no 'correct' way to search the web, but here are a number tips which will help you make your search more efficient.

1 Ignore small words. Search engines tend to ignore them.
2 Ignore capitalization and punctuation, but be careful with spelling.
3 If you use words like 'AND' and 'OR', they must be capitalized for the search engine to identify them as search operators.
4 Using '+' or '-' in front of a term will either include or remove it from a broader search.
5 Use quotation marks to search for an exact phrase.

## Getting organized

The resources of the web are wonderful, but they will not be of much use if you can't find them. Although the history function is useful, it doesn't really help you remember what websites were valuable, or even what they contained. As such, you can end up jumping from one website to another without really exploring what is actually available. Or you might discover a great nugget of material, only to never find it again. To avoid this, it is very important to keep all your valuable resources organized.

### Bookmarking

For organizational reasons, you should **bookmark** (or 'favourite') websites (i.e. ask the browser to remember the website) that are relevant to you. This is normally done in two ways: by clicking on the star icon in the **toolbar** of your browser, or by going to the 'bookmarks' menu and selecting the 'add to bookmarks' command.

Unfortunately, although bookmarks can be a good memory aid, bookmarking can become addictive. Very soon, you may find yourself with an enormous unorganized list of websites you have bookmarked while browsing the web. In many cases, you may not even remember why you chose to bookmark the website in the first place. Luckily, the bookmarks feature also allows you to organize your bookmarks into folders, exactly like those you use to organize documents on your computer.

It is very important to think about how you want to structure your folders before you begin actively adding bookmarks. Decide on a hierarchy. If your course is thematic, the topic may be the top level of the folder structure. You may also choose to bookmark by skill, grammar point, or level. With so much multimedia on the web, it is also very useful to group resources by media type: audio, video, image, text, etc. See if you can come up with a **taxonomy** that fits your needs. The key is to create a taxonomy that is simple and easy to use, but don't worry if the taxonomy isn't perfect straight away. Once you have established a basic structure for your bookmarks, you can change it again at any time by using the 'edit bookmarks' function on your browser to move bookmarks or create and/or move folders. To practice organizing and reorganizing your bookmarks, search the web for guidelines on how to bookmark for your particular browser and follow the procedure described in those guidelines.

---

**Try this** ☞ **Developing a taxonomy**

This is an excellent activity to do with the entire class via an interactive whiteboard (IWB) (see Chapter 10). Explain to your students that a taxonomy is a way of classifying and organizing information in a specific area. This can be a subject area such as English or biology, or even how to manage your photograph collection. Ask your students to think of a taxonomy for language learning and elicit ideas. Using a finger or the IWB pen, students can create a visual representation of the taxonomy in the form of an easily edited mind map which, like a simple file, can be saved to the computer for use at a later date.

## Social bookmarking

The classic way to bookmark websites is helpful, but it has its limitations. Many websites contain information on a number of different subjects that may be relevant to your work, so it can be hard to organize them into folders. The method of social bookmarking, however, offers an alternative.

The key distinction between social bookmarking and traditional bookmarking is that the former is hosted on the web rather than on your computer. That is, traditional bookmarks are stored on your computer's browser and can't be accessed anywhere else. Social bookmarks, however, are stored on a bookmarking website and are accessible on any computer with internet connection. This can very convenient when you need to access your bookmarks on both personal and work computers.

Social bookmarking is built around the concept of **tagging**. Tagging is a way of attaching keywords to a website to help you find it again. Most search engines, for example, are based on some form of tagging system whereby the search engine interprets your search based on a scan of website content. In the case of social bookmarking, you set the tags yourself. Tagging allows you to customize the way your bookmarks are organized and, most importantly, allows you to organize them according to equal multiple criteria. Organization is important here too. The more uniformly you tag, the more likely it is that you will get each relevant website.

In order to create social bookmarks, you need to join a social bookmarking website – an example of which is shown in Screenshot 3.1.

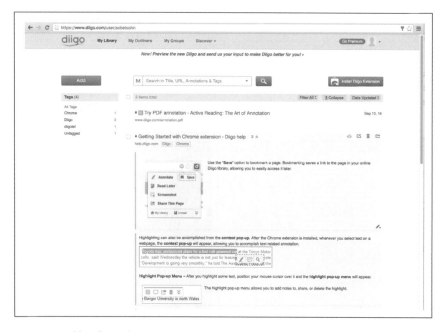

SCREENSHOT 3.1    *Diigo social bookmarking site*

Once you have joined a social bookmarking website, your existing bookmarks will be automatically imported to your account. To add new bookmarks, you can create a button that will appear in the toolbar of your browser. Each time you see a website you want to bookmark, click on this button. Add tags to new bookmarks by typing your keywords into the dialogue box that appears under the name of the website. You can also add and edit tags by clicking on a bookmark in your collection and selecting 'edit', to bring up a tag field. To make tagging more precise, you can:

- browse existing tags
- separate tags by spaces
- combine general tags (e.g. 'EFL') with more specific criteria such as language level ('A1'), language point ('present perfect') and age group ('teenagers').

## RSS feeds

Really simple syndication (RSS) feeds are another great way to help you keep up with the ever-changing content on the internet. You've probably seen the symbol for RSS on lots of websites you visit regularly (see Figure 3.1).

FIGURE 3.1    *RSS symbol*

When you sign up to a website with RSS, it means you can receive automatic notifications on all of the new updates to that website directly, instead of having to manually log on to each individual website and searching for what is new. That is, RSS feeds bring the information to you, allowing you to keep up to date effortlessly.

In order to access RSS content, you need to sign up for a **reader** which collects the content from multiple websites and displays it on one website, just for you (see Screenshot 3.2). Most readers are available for free on the web.

SCREENSHOT 3.2    *RSS feeds on a reader page*

For advanced students of English, RSS feeds offer an excellent opportunity to individualize content, promote autonomous learning, and provide opportunities for extensive reading.

Once you have logged on to the reader, you can add RSS feeds by pasting the web address directly into it (look for a button that says 'add subscriptions'). However, it is easier to add feeds from the selected websites themselves. Nowadays, most serious blogging websites as well as magazines, newspapers, and other media have buttons linking to an RSS reader. If you click on the button, a set of icons will appear with a list of readers. Click on your reader's icon and the RSS feed will be set up in your reader. This makes it easy to add feeds as you browse the web – but be careful not to create complete chaos! Organize your feeds into folders and think twice before adding one. Is it something you will read every day? Your reader will also have numerous settings you can use to control how your feeds appear. Explore them once you feel comfortable with the general functions.

## Search-based activities

More than anything else, the web is a repository of information. Students can research virtually anything under the sun. If something exists in real life, you will certainly find something relating to it online. Here is a trio of search-based activities which work well in the language classroom, as well as two activities related to a museum field trip.

**Try this** ☞ **Job applications**

There are thousands of job search websites on the web. Some are general (such as Monster and Indeed), while others focus on specific job markets (such as TotallyLegal and SimplyLaw which focus on careers in law). To introduce the topic of job applications, review jobs and careers with your class. Ask students if they have ever attended a job interview. What kinds of questions were they asked? Write a variety of job titles on strips of paper and place them in a hat. Split the class into pairs and ask each pair to choose one strip of paper. Give each pair access to a job search website and tell them to search for the job title that they chose. Ask them to print out and read the job description. Then get them to role-play an interview for the job, with one student playing the interviewer and the other the applicant. You could also video the students' role-plays.

As an alternative activity, get students to write their CVs and draft an application for a real job of their choice.

**Try this** ☞ **Virtual tours**

Not everybody has the time or money to take a trip to an exotic part of the world. However, the web provides students with the ability to take virtual tours of popular landmarks and cities. In fact, virtual tours appeal to the same physical mode of learning as if you were physically there. Put students into small groups and ask each group to search for a landmark or city in a different part of the world. To make this easier, prepare a list of suggestions of places for which you know virtual tours exist. Tell students to go on the tour themselves and to take notes about interesting things they see or hear. Get students to present their findings to the class.

**Try this** ☞ **Museums**

Many museums offer interactive websites which allow you to search their collections and even create your own personal gallery. Students can simply browse a museum's website and choose their favourite object for their own gallery. You can also assign specific search tasks, such as finding a painting by a specific artist or looking for an example of a particular art genre.

**Try this** ☞ **Field trip (1): Art descriptions**

Split your class into small groups. Get each group to choose a work of art from the museum. Together they write a description of the work. Collect the descriptions and put them in a hat. Each group then chooses a description and searches the museum's website to find the corresponding piece.

**Try this** ☞ **Field trip (2): Art comparisons**

Ask your students to find works of art that share certain features or subjects, for example landscapes of mountains, portraits of women, still lifes with chairs. Students then compare their selected works of art. This can lead to interesting discussions of art genres and history.

## Google Earth

One particularly exciting tool to use for visual tours is Google Earth. Google Earth is a program you can install on your device which provides static satellite pictures of nearly every corner of the world. Type in a location, such as Paris, and you can get satellite views that are detailed enough for you to see people and cars on a street. You can also get a macro-view of the entire world. Google Earth comes with a variety of fun sub-tools, including those which allow you to see selected cities in 3D and to see cities through views of street scenes as if you were walking the streets yourself.

Google Sky is another great app which maps the universe as far as we know it. A particularly interesting feature superimposes the constellations on a night sky and could be used as an introduction to stories and myths.

For a full list of the tools available, go to www.google.com and search for 'Google tools'. Google adds new tools on a regular basis, so check the website regularly.

---

**Try this** ☞  **Google Earth**

Use Google Earth as a whole-class IWB-based activity for giving directions. Hand out maps to your students, e.g. a map of London. Then open Google Earth and search for 'London'. Invite a student to the front of the class and give them the IWB pen. Let the class direct the student to a particular point of interest, e.g. Regent's Park. The student can use the pen to zoom in and move along actual city streets until they reach the location.

---

**Try this** ☞  **Great place to live**

Get students to search for, and zoom in on, towns and cities in Google Earth. Ask them to pick one of the towns/cities as their 'dream home', where they would love to live. Ask them if they can think of any objective criteria for what makes a town/city a great place to live and write their ideas on the board. Explain that there are websites which rank towns/cities by their 'liveability'. Give the class the web address of one of these websites (which you can find before class by searching for 'towns/cities liveability'). Go over the liveability criteria listed on the website with the class. Are they the same as the students' ideas? In pairs or small groups, the students can study the rankings of different towns/cities and find what position their dream town/city occupies. They can then prepare and present their findings, using presentation software such as PowerPoint, wikis, or blogs.

---

**Try this** ☞  **Around the world on €5,000**

Tell students to imagine that they each have a budget of €5,000 and a list of cities that they have to visit in a limited time period. Get students to locate the cities on Google Earth, explore the region, and look for interesting structures or geographical features. Then log on to a travel website and create an itinerary which stays on time and within budget. Ask each student (or group of students) to compare their results.

## WebQuests

**WebQuests** are structured, web-based activities which are excellent examples of 'enquiry-based learning'. Unlike search-based activities (discussed above), where the core focus is on <u>finding</u> information (e.g. the distance between two cities), WebQuests are centred on <u>using</u> information for a specific purpose in relation to higher-order thinking skills, such as comparing, analyzing, or evaluating. In other words, the search is not an end in itself but part of the means to solving a problem or supporting an argument.

Well-designed WebQuests encourage technology integration, where the lines between the computer and the classroom lesson blur. If you are in the fortunate position of having access to a computer lab, you can quickly get your students to collect information on the internet and then ask them to return to their seats to complete their tasks offline. The web-based search component of the WebQuest need not take long; by giving students clear instructions and websites on where to visit, students can find the information they need in a matter of minutes.

One of the greatest challenges for language students using the web lies in one of the web's greatest strengths – its authenticity. Although there are lots of websites aimed at language learners, most WebQuests involve the use of websites with ungraded language.

 *Getting it right*

**Pre-selecting websites for WebQuests**

Consider the following when pre-selecting websites for WebQuests.

- Accessibility: How quickly can the students access the information? Real content should never be more than three clicks away.
- Language level: Is the information at a level your students will understand? Is the information supported with pictures, sound, or other kinds of scaffolding?
- Age appropriacy: Is the content on the website appropriate for the age of your students?

## Steps in a WebQuest

Traditional WebQuests that are used in mainstream first language education often have a prescribed structure. While you certainly do not need to follow the steps in this structure exactly, they do serve as a good reference point when designing a web-based search activity. Create and post your own set of steps on a website, or print and hand them out to students in class. Be sure to discuss each step with students in detail so that they understand what will happen and what you expect.

### 1 Present the context/scenario

Before your students get started, put the task into context. You can do this orally or in written form, as part of a worksheet or using a website. If, for example, the subject to explore is the weather, then brainstorm weather vocabulary and ask students about climates around the world. This will spark their interest and get the class focused.

### 2 Explain the task

Once students are interested in the topic, it's time to discuss the task. Be very clear about the overall goals. A WebQuest should be more than a series of questions with answers available on the web. Continuing with the weather example, the task may be to research weather in two countries and create a presentation comparing conditions.

Note that WebQuests are task- and content-driven and are not activities generally associated with promoting accuracy. However, it is possible to create very specific criteria for presentations and worksheets, which will generate defined chunks of language.

### 3 Explain the steps

After students have been introduced to the goals, it's time to go over the specific steps they will need to follow to reach these goals. Most successful WebQuests feature a logical sequence of targeted questions through which students gather information to solve the overall task. Most teachers prefer to assign specific websites for students to explore, as this cuts down on random search time. On the other hand, allowing the students to make their own search choices can strengthen critical thinking.

### 4 Explain the product and assessment

Define the final outcome of the WebQuest. Will you require an oral presentation, a PowerPoint presentation, an essay, a wiki, or a blog post? How will this final product be evaluated? Since the WebQuest consists of process and product in equal proportions, you will need to take both into consideration when assigning a grade. A clear instruction or rubric is generally the best way to do this. The rubric criteria will depend on the process and product of your WebQuest, and the overall language aims you seek to achieve through the activity. There are many free rubric generators available on the web which can make the process of developing a rubric fast and easy (see *Useful websites*).

**Try this** ☞ **Restaurateur**

Tell students to imagine that they are an entrepreneur and want to open a restaurant in the city of Dublin. What kind of restaurant will it be? Where will it be located? They can research locations, buildings, menu designs, and recipes to include on their menu on the web.

**Try this** ☞ **Relocation**

Ask students to imagine that they want to move to a new city. They have to find out the best areas to live and identify houses on the market, choosing one they like within a set budget. Get students to prepare a short presentation on their chosen house, explaining why they like it and what makes it ideal for them to relocate to.

**Try this** ☞ **The greatest team ever**

Get students to imagine that they are the manager of a new international sports team (e.g. football, volleyball, basketball, etc.). Ask them to investigate players from past events (e.g. World Cups) and put together the greatest team ever. They should choose no more than three players from one country. Get them to explain who their choices are and why.

**Try this** ☞ **The greatest inventions ever**

Ask your students to research inventions and select five that they feel are the most important in history. Alternatively, get students to search the web for the most 'useless' inventions in history, or inventions that have been bad for mankind. Their task is then to explain why they feel their chosen inventions were important, useless, or bad.

## Polls and surveys

Polls and surveys are excellent tools. Polls are generally quick, one-question ways to get information on a single topic. Surveys are more complex and may contain multiple questions. They generate lots of targeted language practice, encourage critical thinking, and, on a more basic level, provide rich and controversial material for discussions. There are endless examples of polls and surveys available on the internet, so should you decide not to create one of your own, most poll/survey creation websites will have a directory of ready-made ones that you can search through to find one that suits your needs. Serious surveys record public opinion on matters ranging from politics to economics, to consumer tastes. Less serious polls can include questions such as 'Are you ticklish?' and 'Would you ever get a tattoo?' In short, anything anyone might have an opinion on can be turned into a poll or survey.

Most language teachers agree that using authentic and personalized materials improves motivation. Using polls and surveys has the added benefit of developing critical thinking skills and the language used to compare and contrast, analyze, summarize, and evaluate.

To familiarize yourself with polls and surveys, experiment by creating a survey on a survey creation website (see *Useful websites*). Create a survey about a topic of your choice featuring at least five questions, using all of the question types available on the website. Send the survey's web address to a select group of students or colleagues and, once they have completed it, check the results.

### Using existing polls and surveys

Students can search for surveys and polls on the web according to their personal areas of interest. To find a survey on a specific topic, e.g. football, a search with the words 'survey' and 'football' should give you some useful results. In many cases, students can even participate in the polls and surveys you find as well as analyze the existing data. As a long-term project, your students can follow polls and surveys over a period of time and note any changes they observe.

### Creating your own poll or survey

Collecting data manually can be a time-consuming task. You will need to ask yourself if the work involved in setting up a survey or poll will take time away from other classroom activities. And to what extent is the preparatory work linked to learning English?

Survey creation tools online simplify the creation process and allow you to use your classroom time to focus on the immediate language task. There are numerous choices on the web, many of them free. Most allow you to create a variety of question types using multiple choice, rating scales, or open text fields. You can even add picture prompts to questions. The surveys can be sent via email or made available on a website, for instance as part of a blog post or wiki. Free survey creation tools have some limitations, in terms of the number of questions and responses per individual survey, but they are robust enough to serve most classroom needs. See Screenshot 3.3 for an example of a simple survey created using SurveyMonkey (see *Useful websites*).

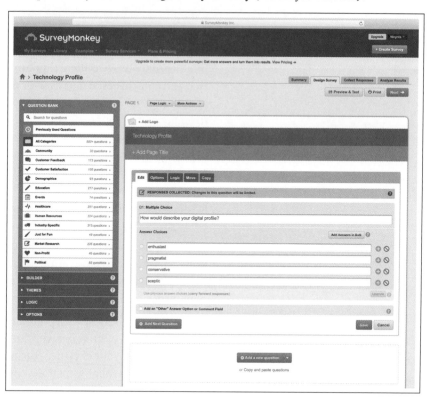

SCREENSHOT 3.3    *SurveyMonkey quiz*

Once participants have responded to the survey, the website evaluates the responses and provides an automatic report which you can either display to the class online or print out for students to read (see Screenshot 3.4).

Many poll and survey ideas will come directly from the content of your coursebook. Units on food may well suggest a survey on students' likes and dislikes. A unit on greetings and salutations could lead to a cross-cultural survey on customs and traditions. Polls and surveys can be conducted in your class, throughout your school, or across the world. They can form part of a broader cultural exchange or 'twinning' project where two or more schools collaborate on virtual projects (they are really useful as conversation starters).

Polls and surveys can be successfully used in assessment, especially for student self-assessment purposes. At the beginning of the school year, you can create a learning styles and student reflection questionnaire. Students can answer questions about how they learn best and what their priorities are for the new school year. This information can be evaluated for the entire class and help you decide how to approach your lessons. You can also use online surveys to allow students to evaluate you and your work and help you in your professional development. (See Chapter 8 for more ideas on using poll/survey tools for evaluating student progress.)

SCREENSHOT 3.4    *Survey report*

## Cloud computing

One of the most significant developments of the last ten years is the growth of **cloud computing**. The cloud is nothing mysterious. It is none other than the internet itself. It is now possible to offer products online with the overall increase in, and reach of, high-speed internet connections and more powerful **bandwidth**. Bandwidth is similar to a road: the less traffic there is, the more smoothly and rapidly it flows. An increase in traffic, however, will cause traffic jams and delays. Instead of installing software packages on your computer, the same programs are now available through your browser. This is known as **software as a service**.

Such online programs are often known as 'web apps'. If you use webmail, such as Gmail or Yahoo! Mail, you are using a web app. Your email messages are not saved on the specific device you are using but hosted on a server somewhere on the internet, which you can access from any device connected to the internet.

There is a huge variety of web apps available today. In fact, the most popular software providers now offer web versions of their popular tools. Microsoft, for example, offers their Office suite (e.g. Word, PowerPoint, and Excel) entirely online. Even complete learning management systems can be found in the cloud.

When working with web apps, rather than buying a software license tied to one or more computers, you purchase a subscription to a service. There is nothing to download to your computer. This is generally a much cheaper alternative to buying software. In fact, in many cases you may not need to pay anything at all to use a web app. It also reduces the need to buy expensive hardware, since most devices can provide access to web apps, although there are some which only operate on a specific operating system, such as Apple iOS or Android. But there is almost always a similar alternative on the system you are using.

Google Docs, Google Slides, and Google Sheets are free alternatives to Microsoft Word, PowerPoint, and Excel. Using Google Docs, for example, you can collaborate on a cloud-based document with colleagues in real time, posting comments and communicating via the 'chat' function. The program offers rich templates and most of the functionality of expensive word processing programs.

Google Docs, Google Slides, and Google Sheets are part of a larger integrated collection of web apps for communication and collaboration which Google has bundled for schools under the title 'The Google Apps for Education Suite' (see Screenshot 3.5). This integrated solution is targeted at schools and organizations and includes Google Classroom – a tool which helps you to create classes, enrol students, and monitor their work.

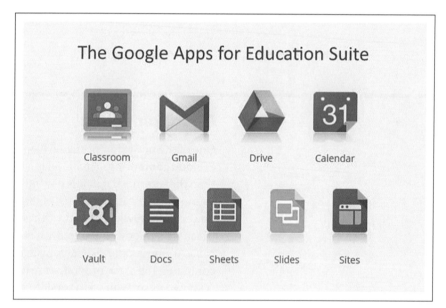

SCREENSHOT 3.5    *Google Apps for Education*

One great advantage of the cloud is the ability to save your data online. With cloud-based data storage, CDs, DVDs, bulky hard drives, and USB sticks that can be easy to lose are no longer necessary. You can also share all of your data with others without having to send emails with attachments. There are many options for storing data online. If you are working with Google Apps,

Google Drive is the obvious solution, as Google Docs, Slides, and Sheets are automatically saved here. Apple also provides an alternative with iCloud. Another well-known alternative is Dropbox. In all three cases, basic storage is available free of charge, with more memory available for a small fee.

It is also possible to back up your entire system to the cloud. Cloud back-up services operate in the background when you are online, protecting you from catastrophic data loss should something happen to your device.

Some people have concerns about saving data online. There is, for instance, a legitimate fear that someone could try to steal their data. While data storage services are generally very secure, nothing on the internet is without security risk. It is important that you protect your data with very strong passwords and security settings (see Chapter 2 for more information on internet security).

# 4 Email and instant messaging

## Email

Due to the fact that email lies somewhere between written and oral language, it presents interesting writing challenges. It is less formal than a letter but certainly more structured than a text message. Emails are usually relatively short. If you want to send a long message, it is better to include it as an attachment, which is less likely to get corrupted and can also be stored more easily by the recipient.

Email is an **asynchronous learning** tool – that is, people do not have to be online at the same time to communicate with each other. This has certain distinct advantages over instant messaging (discussed below), which is a **synchronous learning** tool where communication takes place in real time, like face-to-face interactions. Instant messaging requires a higher degree of fluency to be effective, so it can be a huge challenge to lower-level language learners. In addition, email communication is easier to organize for teachers. Since there is no need to arrange a specific time to be online to communicate with a partner, email projects can be flexibly scheduled and even conducted from one computer, if necessary.

Instant messaging has overtaken email as the main method of online social communication. However, email remains the dominant tool for 'official' communication – both professionally and in a school environment. Email has been a key tool in twinning projects. However, now that there are more flexible web-based tools in the form of wikis and social networks (see Chapters 5 and 6), the role of email in such projects is diminishing. Working on projects in tandem via email is always an individual experience, whether the email is sent to a group or one student, as the documents are not anchored in any shared space. With wikis and social networks, the collaborative work facility is centralized. The participants in a project are pulled to the wiki website to access and edit information. It acts like a magnet, drawing all of the participants to one place, whereas email involves sending (pushing) information from one place to another or to many other places (i.e. from one participant's email account to that of one or more other participants). Nevertheless, email still has a role to play in establishing initial communication, and it offers a no-frills, stripped-down way to get started.

**Try this** ☞ **Same life, different location**

In this project, students link with a corresponding school in another country. The school may be in an English-speaking country or, as an interesting alternative, it could involve schools in two non-English-speaking countries communicating through the medium of English. The goal of the project is to compare the lives of students and reflect on the similarities and differences they find.

This project can be carried out on a number of different levels. Some points to compare are:

- daily schedules
- subjects studied
- living spaces
- popular culture
- free time.

Each student can choose one aspect of life to work on and then exchange documents with a partner from the corresponding school. As a final step, students can write a paragraph outlining how their life would change if they were to trade places.

**Try this** ☞ **Story circles**

Before class, make a numbered list of your students. Write the first sentence of a story (e.g. *Sarah didn't go to school on Friday.*) in the body of an email, and send it to the first student on the list. This student writes the next sentence in the story and then forwards the email to the next student on the list, and so on, until every student has had a chance to write a sentence. Continue with another round if the students are still interested and/or if the story is not yet complete. Print out copies of the story for your students. In pairs, have students edit the story for language errors. Finally, go over the errors with the class.

This is also a good activity to use at the start of a twinning project, as it allows students to collaborate on a shared piece of work without the pressure of having to communicate with each other directly.

## Dialogue journals

Email is a particularly useful medium for setting up dialogue journals – essentially, written conversations between two people. Observations have shown that, because email is less governed by rules of style, students tend to write more compared to conventional paper-and-pencil tasks. Also, because email can be restricted to a limited audience, it is a safe place for students to practise and gain confidence before moving on to a more public forum, such as a blog or wiki (see Chapter 5).

Student–teacher dialogue journals generally begin with a question. When starting out with a dialogue journal, make the question very concrete, e.g. *What is your favourite food?* You can then comment on the response and add a follow-up question or introduce a new topic. Once the student feels confident responding, ask them to choose a topic. Another option is to use the dialogue journal as a feedback element on the class materials or teaching methods.

## Instant messaging

Instant messaging is a synchronous activity: at least two people must be online simultaneously in order to chat in real time. Instant messaging usually has the feel of face-to-face conversations, distinguishing it from email which is usually more formal. Traditionally, instant messaging was text-based and conducted in chat rooms: essentially, you read messages by other users in the same 'room' and responded. Chat rooms were organized according to various criteria: common interest (sports, language learning, technology, etc.), age, or geographical location.

**Try this** ☞   **Instant messaging brainstorm session**

Use instant messaging to conduct a brainstorming session when introducing a topic. For example, for 'global social awareness' you might use instant messaging to brainstorm different uses of water. The advantage of using instant messaging is that you can save the transcript and thus capture the students' thinking process.

### Videoconferencing

Today, although chat rooms in themselves are less common, instant messaging has become far more diverse. Videoconferencing apps such as Skype now include embedded instant messaging, allowing participants to talk via video and send text-based messages at the same time. These multimedia chats allow students to use all the options at once, which will stimulate and challenge higher-level students. They do not have to toggle between text, sound, and video. They can listen via headphones, speak into a microphone, watch the webcam, and read instant messages, all at the same time. They also allow lower-level students to participate using just one of the options that they feel comfortable with.

As mentioned earlier, synchronous communication can be difficult for language learners. It makes little sense to have your students spend a great deal of time online simply thinking before typing a response to a post. However, voice and video chats relieve students of the burden of writing and allow for real spoken communication across countries and continents.

**Try this** ☞   **Debates**

Brainstorm debate topics with your class and agree on one to follow up in an online debate. To make it more exciting, invite students from another class (or even another school) to join you in an online debate at a mutually convenient time. Before the debate, email round a list of those students who are going to debate 'for' and who are going to debate 'against' the motion so that on the day it is clear who is doing what. Prepare some keywords and phrases that your students might need, and go through these in class before the online debate. Make sure that your debate has a clear end time, and that you are on hand to intervene if either side of the debate runs out of ideas or the debate starts going off track.

**Try this** ☞ **Radio plays**

Students collaborate online and write a script for a radio play. During the course of a series of voice-chat sessions (which could be in class time), the actors can practise their show and then invite a broader audience to the final performance, all online.

**Try this** ☞ **Question time with a twinned school**

Prepare for a 'live' interview between twinned school students. First, ensure that each student has access to a device with internet connection and videoconferencing equipment (webcam, headphones, and a microphone). Agree on the theme of the interview (e.g. 'my daily routine') with the counterpart teacher in the twinned school, and put students into pairs by matching one of your students with one from the twinned school, so that it is clear on the day who will be chatting to whom. In class, ask your students to prepare ten questions for the interview on the chosen theme, as well as answers to questions that their partner might ask them. On the day of the interview, get students to note down as many differences between their own daily routine and their partner's.

# 5 Blogs, wikis, podcasts, and video

## Blogs

Of all the new web-based technologies, blogs are probably one of the most common and accepted. They are practical, easy to use, and require only basic technology skills to create and manage.

A blog is an web-based journal where users post their thoughts, opinions, and hobby endeavours on a regular basis. Blog posts are traditionally organized by date, most recent to oldest, although it is possible to follow posts by subject tags as well.

Blogs can be written by individuals, groups, or organizations. They can also be used to host discussions or projects. In a blog, the author shares opinions, insights, and hyperlinks to related websites of interest.

One key feature of a blog is the comment function. Only the author of a blog can edit a post, but anyone who has permission to access the blog can comment on what the blogger has written, or reply to the comments of other readers. This makes a blog dynamic and ever-changing, unlike a website, which tends to remain in one constant state for an extended period of time. For those who prefer not to get feedback, the comment function can be turned off in the settings menu of the blog. Alternatively, as author you can also filter which readers can view responses, in much the same way you can control who sees your Facebook posts.

In education, there are four key types of blogs:

1 **Teacher blogs:** These can be used to communicate with students and provide hyperlinks to resources. For example, the teacher can post homework assignments and hyperlinks to useful resources. The teacher can also use a blog to manage resources and share them with both local colleagues and those around the world.

2 **Student blogs:** Students can use blogs for a variety of writing assignments. They can be managed as the focus of projects by individual students (for example, in the form of an e-portfolio) or by small groups. True to the original intention of blogs, students can also use blogs to record and share their reflections with the teacher and their peers.

3 **Class blogs:** These are blogs for the whole class. They are particularly useful in twinning projects. A class blog can be hyperlinked to both student blogs and teacher blogs.

4 **Project or topic blogs:** Blogs need not only be defined by their authors – the subject of a blog is equally important. You can create a blog for a specific topic or a project. The blog can be ongoing, or you can simply delete it when the project is over or when you move on to a

different topic. Blogs are not designed to be permanent, and you can delete and create as many blogs as you like.

To start a blog, go to one of the blog-building websites available free on the internet (for some suggestions, see *Useful websites*). Each website has a step-by-step guide for you to follow. Screenshot 5.1 shows an example of a blog created by a teacher, trainer, and materials writer based in the UK who uses it to communicate with fellow professionals around the world.

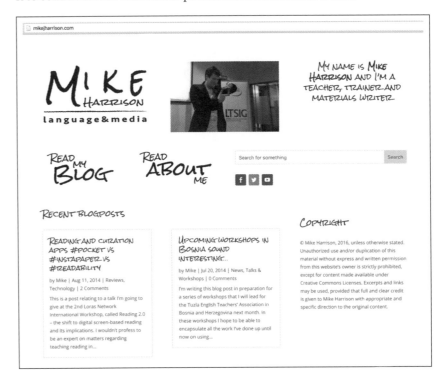

SCREENSHOT 5.1    *Teacher's blog*

The following are examples of activities involving the use of blogs which have worked in EFL classrooms in different parts of the world. What value can you see in using blogs for these activities?

Try this 👉 **Overpaid or underpaid?**

Review the vocabulary of jobs with your students. Ask them what career they would like to pursue when they have finished their education. If your students are advanced, explore the rationale for their decision. Is it the money they can earn or the satisfaction the job brings? Ask your students if they feel every job gets paid fairly. Get each student to write a blog post on the class blog, focusing on one job that is overpaid and one that is underpaid and to explain why they feel this is so. Each student must then read and comment on at least three of their classmates' blogs.

Try this 👉 **Language learning journal**

Assign a weekly blogging task to your students, asking them to talk about their learning for the week. What did they learn? What was difficult? What did they particularly enjoy? Blogs are excellent tools for reflection on learning and, as long as you are clear about how often you check them, are a good way to encourage students to write.

**Try this** 👉 **Favourite sports stars**

Get students to write about their favourite sports stars on their student blogs, and ask them to provide hyperlinks to related websites of interest. They can then post updates and comments on recent events that their sports stars were involved in, and invite other students to voice their opinions.

# Wikis

A wiki is a website which allows users to work together to add and edit content. They are collaborative, built up and maintained by multiple users.

## Wikipedia

As an introduction, it is useful to go to the mother of all wikis: Wikipedia (see *Useful websites*). Wikipedia is an enormous collection of information, editable by anyone who registers to the website. The users building it up are international. As anyone can edit the content, though, teachers and students have to remember to check the information against other sources when using it for work, to ensure that the facts are accurate.

**Try this** 👉 **Checking Wikipedia**

Direct students to Wikipedia. Together, explore how you can register and edit a page. Explain to students that you want them to look for information about their home country or town, and to check whether what is written is true. If the information they find is true, they can add new details to it. If it is not true, they can correct it. Make sure to tell the students that they must be factually accurate in their edits and must not knowingly post incorrect information or nonsense. Check Wikipedia periodically to see if anyone has edited your students' posts. They can even write a new Wikipedia page on a subject they feel they know a lot about.

## The structure of wikis

The structure of a wiki is extremely simple. It starts off as a blank page, and is developed by adding text and hyperlinking additional pages. These additional pages can belong to the wiki, or they can be external website, and they are hyperlinked to each other and/or a homepage. This is as easy as a click on the wiki toolbar (consult your particular wiki for guidelines). Screenshots 5.2 and 5.3 are of a personal wiki that was created on a team collaboration service website, Wikispaces (see *Useful websites*). Other wiki-building tools may have slightly different terminology, but the basic structures are very similar. Their simplicity makes it easy to create and keep track of smaller wikis yourself, for use with your students.

In Screenshot 5.2 we are in 'view' mode, which displays what the wiki currently looks like. If we click on 'changes' in the 'Home' panel on the right of the screen, we will also see a list of all the other previous versions of the page which we can view. Below the main content on the page, there is also a comments box and on the right, there is a button to create a new page. The new page can then be hyperlinked to any other page on your wiki or, for that matter, to any other website on the world wide web.

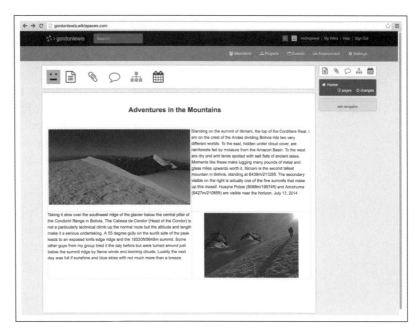

SCREENSHOT 5.2    *Wiki in 'view' mode*

Screenshot 5.3 shows the wiki in 'edit' mode. Here, there is a toolbar much like the one in a conventional word processing program. One very powerful addition to the toolbar, however, is the facility for adding widgets to your page. Some enhancements which are good to start off with are audio or video clips and photos. At the top of the screen, you save your page with the save button. It then becomes the most recent version you will see in view mode.

SCREENSHOT 5.3    *Wiki in 'edit' mode*

## Wikis and the writing process

A wiki allows all of its users to collaborate on a page, saving different versions as the text is developed. For this reason, it can be a useful tool to support group 'process writing'. Process writing breaks down a writing task into manageable steps, providing students with a structure to follow. Traditionally, there are five phases in the writing process. These have been identified below.

1  **Brainstorm:** This is when the students all contribute their ideas on a topic, to warm up for the task. This phase has no structure; it is for idea-sharing. With wikis, students can create a group brainstorming page for a project. Students can log on and add, edit, or delete ideas without the risk of losing what their peers have created. The teacher can also add comments to the page.

2  **Draft:** This is the phase where students start organizing their ideas from the brainstorming phase into coherent text. This may be just an outline or a full first draft. The 'history' function for saving multiple versions encourages students to take more risks at this stage in their writing, since they know they can easily modify their text later, and go back to a previous version if necessary.

3  **Revise:** The revision phase is for feedback on the piece of text being written. This feedback can come from a teacher or another student who has been assigned the role of editor. On a wiki, the editor can either use the comment function or make edits to the text itself.

4  **Edit:** Here the focus is on editing for accuracy – getting spelling correct, making sure appropriate punctuation is being used, etc. The teacher or student editor can edit a page of work and simply highlight errors for correction which the author then reworks, making the appropriate changes. Participants can then go back and review the process step-by-step using the 'history' tab.

5  **Publish:** Finally, when the text is ready to be published, there is no need to **upload** it to a school website or other location, as the wiki itself is the website. Students can make last-minute adjustments to the format without fear of making irreversible changes. You can decide who to give access to the wiki – your class alone, parents/carers, teachers, your twinned school, etc.

## Class wiki website

As a teacher, you can use a wiki as a class homepage – a place where you can post messages and assignments as well as provide hyperlinks to resources. You need to create a wiki and then invite all your students (by email) to join. In this way, you are using a wiki to pull your students to a central location. As part of your class wiki, each student can create their own profile page and link them to the class wiki homepage. You can choose how specific to be about the content of your students' profile page (see page 00 for more information on this idea). Wikis can also simply serve as an online place to keep information such as useful hyperlinks, videos and audio clips, student work, and teacher commentary.

---

**Try this** ☞   **What's going on?**

Most major cities have online city guides which list entertainment available in the area (music, art exhibitions, plays, films, etc.). Pre-select a set of city guides for English-speaking cities (or cities which have city guides in English online). Explain to students that they are going to plan a fun Saturday evening in a city.

Elicit categories of activities that can take place in the city and create an empty wiki page for each category. If possible, do this with the class using an IWB or a computer projector to demonstrate the steps. Split the class into groups so that each group can research what is happening in a particular city on a Saturday evening. Assign each group one of the wiki pages you created and ask them to fill it with the information they collected. Invite each group to share their wikis. Compare results between cities. Are their similarities and/or differences?

**Try this** ☞ **Student newspaper wiki**

Bring a newspaper to class and review its structure with the students. If possible, present the website of the same newspaper and compare the structure of each. Explain that you want the class to create an online school newspaper of their own. Decide with the class on sections for your newspaper (sports, news, learning tips, opinions, etc.). Assign student(s) to each section that you've agreed on and ask them to brainstorm story ideas. These could be news reports, interviews, or even editorials. Encourage students to publish at least one story each week for their respective section of the newspaper. The newspaper can be shared with everybody in the school.

✓ *Getting it right*    **Using RSS feeds to save time on wikis**

Most wikis allow you to generate an RSS feed (see Chapter 3). If you are working with ongoing student or class wikis, you can save a lot of time by creating RSS feeds from the individual websites to your account. You can then read all the postings in one place, and even post back without having to open and close multiple websites in your browser.

## Wikis as collections

Wikis are a very practical tool for collecting information on a particular subject. The fact that any registered user can edit pages means that wikis facilitate great online collaborative projects. Of course, there is the risk that contributors might post incorrect information on the wiki. The teacher can note this and either enter a correction or use the information as a teaching point in class. Alternatively, the students can be given autonomy in their collaborative work and be instructed to use the wiki's editing function to exercise control over the content. With the history function of the wiki, there is no risk that correct information will be permanently deleted. Previous versions can be restored at any time.

**Try this** ☞ **How to learn a foreign language wiki**

Elicit examples of learning strategies, for example drawing mind maps to learn vocabulary, and invite your students to organize them into logical categories, such as how to learn grammar or improve reading skills, listening skills, etc. Display an empty wiki on your IWB (or board, using a projector) and invite students (individually or in groups) to take turns adding to the wiki, creating new pages and content, and hyperlinking them together.

**Try this** ☞ **Collaborative vocabulary lists**

Create a wiki for your class and display the empty wiki on the IWB (or board, using a projector). Explain to the class that you are going to create an ongoing

vocabulary list which every student can contribute to. Decide what categories you want to use to organize vocabulary on the wiki. Depending on your classroom situation, your options might be:
- topic area: home, sports, family
- special focus: ESP medical terminology, hospitality
- language area: adjectives, verbs, nouns.

Create an empty wiki page for each vocabulary category. Split the class into small groups and assign each group a wiki page to work on either in class or at home. Later, reassign the wiki pages so that students can contribute to other pages.

### Choosing between a wiki and a blog

Many activities can be done on a blog or on a wiki. The choice depends on where you want to place the emphasis. If you want your students to comment on one central theme, with their comments listed chronologically, choose a blog. If you want the activity to be a project edited by the group, a wiki is better. See Table 5.1 for a summary of the characteristics and differences between wikis and blogs to help you make the right choice.

| Blogs | Wikis |
| --- | --- |
| • Blogs are based on commentary. | • Wikis are based on editing. |
| • Once something is posted on a blog, only the author can edit it. Others can only add comments. | • Anyone can edit anything on a wiki page. |
| • Blogs can be organized chronologically or by topic. | • Wikis have no predetermined structure. |
| • Blogs tend to present a particular point of view and are personal. | • Wikis are the product of multiple inputs, and tend to be factual. |
| • Blogs are useful for spreading information and linking with like-minded people or those with shared interests. | • Wikis are useful for developing internal communities, promoting collaboration, and sharing information. |

TABLE 5.1   *The differences between blogs and wikis*

## Podcasts

**Podcasts** (a term derived from Apple's 'iPod' media player and the word 'broadcast') are short recordings delivered in **MP3** or **MP4** format. Although the term 'vodcast' has also surfaced, in this book 'podcast' is used to encompass both audio and video casts.

Podcasts are different from other recordings. Not only can they be played on desktop computers and laptops, they can also be downloaded to mobile devices such as portable media players, making them easily accessible for both students and teachers. Using a smartphone, iPod, or other small mobile device, you can store literally hundreds of hours of audio and video content, which you can use with your whole class by connecting your device to a TV or audio output.

### Finding podcasts

Since it is so easy to create podcasts, they are appearing in every area of the web. As with most content on the web, there are good and bad podcasts; and since everything can look so professional, it is hard to know which is which at first glance. Hence, broad searches can be hit-and-miss. Conducting some research beforehand can help simplify your search. The first place to look is on one of the larger podcast search websites (see *Useful websites*). Screenshot 5.4 shows a search result using the fairly wide criterion 'podcasts learn english' on Apple iTunes. The search yielded only 38 results, a manageable number to look through.

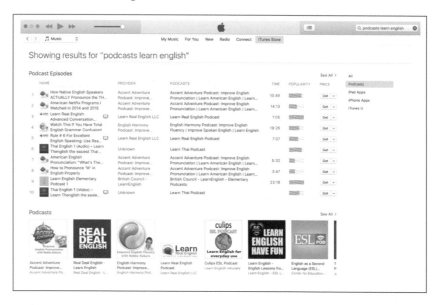

SCREENSHOT 5.4    *Podcast search results on iTunes*

Once you have found a podcast that is useful for you and your students, you have the option to subscribe to the service. Like RSS feeds, podcast subscriptions automatically update your podcast library each time you log in, for example to iTunes or BBC iPlayer. This means that every time you log on to your podcast host, you receive a download of the latest episode of the podcast.

### Creating podcasts

You don't need to be an expert to create your own podcasts. You will find a number of free audio editors on the web. A very popular option in this regard is Audacity (for this and other options, see *Useful websites*). Audacity is an audio editing program which allows you to record audio and then edit it. It also allows you to convert non-digital recordings into digital files. Audacity works much like a traditional recorder with additional tools to help you eliminate background noise and add special effects. Once you have created an audio file, you need to save it – remember that podcasts are saved in the common MP3 or MP4 format. Your audio editor will provide prompts to select the appropriate format.

Pretty much anything you can record can be turned into a podcast. The only limitation is your own imagination. Before you start recording, it's important to plan what you want to say. What will the format of the podcast be? Will it be an interview, a commentary, a report, or maybe even a radio play? What about a game show? How many students will be involved? If possible, make a podcasting project collaborative and encourage students to take turns speaking.

Outline the key talking points, but avoid reading from a script. A podcast in an EFL environment should focus on fluency. Encourage your students to take risks. The recordings can be erased and rerecorded as often as you like.

Once you have a topic and format, you need to be aware of timing. Speaking for two minutes can seem like an eternity for a native speaker, not to mention for a non-native speaker. Limit speaking time for lower-level students to 1–3 minutes maximum. Of course, group podcasts with multiple speakers can be longer.

**Try this** ☞  **This week from classroom X**

This project is based on TV and radio talk shows. Each week, students comment on events of the past week. They can focus on international news, sports, or issues closer to home, such as the topics of their English lessons or what's new in their school. While all students should be encouraged to speak, you will have to limit the number of students actually recording their voices for any given podcast. Split the class into groups and assign each group responsibility for a particular aspect of the podcast. Discuss a commentary format with students. Elicit an organizational structure for a commentary piece and have each group create a clear outline of what they plan to say. Although only one or two students per group will actually speak on the podcast, the whole group will gain valuable speaking practice in the process of preparing for the recording.

**Try this** ☞  **Creative writing podcast**

Get students to practise both creative writing and pronunciation by creating podcasts of their creative writing. Students can write and record themselves reading aloud short stories or poems, and post them online for anyone to listen to. To focus their efforts, you could choose a particular topic for students to write about (for example, 'My perfect holiday'). Alternatively, you could ask students to create spoken images – descriptions of landscapes, people, or scenes. If you or your students like working with online audio tools, you can add background music or record sound effects which you either create yourself or import from relevant websites (see *Useful websites*).

**Try this** ☞  **Trivia show**

Before class, go to a trivia website and choose a series of questions for the game. Explain to students that 'trivia' refers to little known, unusual, and/or unimportant facts. Give a few examples and see if the students can guess the answers. Divide the class into teams of four or five, and assign one student on each team to be the show presenter and the rest show contestants. The presenter leads the show and asks the questions. Use a bell or a kitchen timer to signal the beginning and end of contestants' turns. Ensure that each team has a chance to play the game. Note: when recording the show, be sure to manage the noise level and interruptions.

## Publishing podcasts

One thing to consider is whether you are really planning to make a podcast, or simply a recording of an audio file to play locally from your computer.

Podcasts are meant to be broadcast, and that means they need to get uploaded to a host website. Many students find it particularly rewarding to have a podcast available on the web. There are numerous websites that host podcasts, such as SoundCloud, Blubrry, and Libsyn (see *Useful websites*). Once you have found a place to host your podcast, you can then submit your podcast to iTunes or other popular aggregators, where most people will search.

 *Getting it right*

> **Online safety**
>
> Make sure you tell students of the importance of online safety before asking them to upload content to any online environment. Areas to cover include using 'private' and 'unlisted' options when posting videos, reporting and blocking abusive users, disabling or removing the 'comments' function, and responding to personal messages cautiously. Also remind them that they should not post potentially offensive or explicit material themselves.

# Video

Nowhere has the impact of technology in education been greater than in the area of video. The ability to create and consume video is transforming the way we learn. Use of video can extend the classroom like no other medium, bringing the world and all its knowledge into your classroom and bringing your classroom to the world. Video apps are as far-reaching as your imagination and there are numerous books (such as *Online Video* in this series), websites, and, of course, videos, which provide you with detailed, step-by-step procedures and inspiration. Throughout this book are references to activities involving video. Here is an overview to introduce you to the opportunities.

## Using videos

When thinking of videos, it is useful to categorize them into particular genres. One helpful way of looking at this is to distinguish between the following.

1  **Professional videos:** These can be film clips, television programmes, adverts, etc. Many commercial websites aimed at language learners, e.g. English Central and Voxy (see *Useful websites*), have licensed these kinds of videos and have created lesson plans and activities around them. Note that most of these websites charge a fee.
2  **Instructional videos:** These are created especially for learning. These videos are often components of coursebook series.
3  **User-generated videos:** These are amateur videos posted on websites such as YouTube, from all around the world. They are searchable and can be ranked by popularity.

The easiest way to use video is simply to go online and access the clips where they are hosted. As long as you have decent bandwidth, there is really no need for you to download a video to your local device. Instead, you can stream the video directly from the website where it is hosted. You can play a video via a projector or IWB for a whole-class activity, or use a video as a prompt for an individual activity that students can work on outside of class.

**Try this** 👉 **Silent video**

Play a short section of a video without sound. Ask students to create their own script based on what they see. Play the video again with sound and check how similar the students' scripts are to the original dialogue.

**Try this** 👉 **Name that clip**

Show your students an excerpt from a video. Ask them to come up with a title for the clip. Play the rest of the clip. Ask the class if they would stick with their title and why. Alternatively, give the students the title of a video and ask them to predict the content.

## Embedding

Embedding lets you take a video from one website, such as YouTube or Vimeo, and paste it into another website, blog, social network, PowerPoint presentation, or even a word processing document (see Screenshot 5.5). What was once a cumbersome and confusing process is now as easy as a click of a mouse.

SCREENSHOT 5.5   *YouTube share and embed*

 **Getting it right**   **Copyright**

Copyright issues were discussed in Chapter 2, but video-sharing websites have their own specific rules to consider. Most people who post video to YouTube can be very eager for you to use their videos, as each 'view' increases their popularity. A video that goes 'viral' – spreading around the world with incredible speed – can earn the owner a lot of money. If you see the 'share' button activated on a YouTube video, you can assume the owner wants you to use it. However, you can't always be sure that the owner followed copyright law. In most cases, if you are using the video for educational purposes, you should be complying with the law. YouTube and Google have rich documentation on copyright law, including hyperlinks to content that is guaranteed to be without restrictions (see Chapter 2).

## Creating video

### Basic video

With mobile technology, video is literally in the palm of everybody's hands. Smartphones can record videos of such crispness and detail that they look professionally created. Students and teachers can create video on the go, anytime and anywhere. The videos themselves can be saved on the device, or uploaded to a video-sharing website or social network.

Video can be a good alternative for students who may be shy and/or struggle with writing but can express themselves well orally. Video does not need to be recorded live in front of an audience, yet it is authentic and immediate. Students can practise, record, erase, and try again without feeling the pressure of performing in class. Video also gives students who may be reluctant to participate in class the chance to express themselves in a safe environment, away from the eyes of their classmates.

**Try this** ☞ **Create a 'how-to' video**

Everybody has something they can do well. Ask students to create a 'how-to' video to share with the class. The video could show how to fix a bicycle tyre, how to dance to salsa music, how to play chess, etc. This is a good critical thinking exercise which requires students to break down activities into steps while focusing on describing a process.

### Video slideshow apps

Video slideshow apps allow you to create multimedia slideshows, as opposed to traditional PowerPoint presentations which create 'static' slides. You can combine your own pictures, text, music, and video clips to create professional-looking presentations in minutes. You can upload files saved on your device, or from your social network accounts such as YouTube, Instagram, and Facebook (see Chapter 6). The app itself also has a list of themes, music, and animations for you to choose from, as well as the ability to record a voiceover to create a complete presentation. Video slideshows are a fun way to create video content with very little preparation and with immediate results. The video slideshows themselves are saved in the cloud and can be made available to anybody. Most video slideshow apps offer free basic services but charge fees for additional or enhanced services. (See *Useful websites* for some good options.)

**Try this** ☞ **Create an advert**

Have your students select a product or service and create a video slideshow presentation to promote it. This can also be a group project. The students need to identify the advantages of the product/service and develop a compelling script, using creative language to 'sell' the product/service to their peers.

## Interactive video

Video tuition has become a thriving industry, led by companies such as Khan Academy, which combines whiteboard instruction and online video to create a virtual classroom which can be accessed on demand.

Of course, you can follow this model and upload your own lessons. By uploading videos of lessons, your students can explore content before they get to class, catch up on a lesson if they were absent, and use the videos to review content at a later date. The content could be a slideshow video as described above, or a simple clip that you would like to work with in class. Either way, integrating video can free up valuable class time to focus on language production. Record a grammar explanation or simply create a video of yourself introducing a concept. If you are starting a class project, you could record instructions for the class. Using video in this way, you are relieving yourself of the burden of always presenting content in class, and are encouraging students to think and work autonomously.

While this is great in itself, emerging technologies let you move beyond the one-way passive consumption model to a truly interactive experience. Technologies such as Playposit (see *Useful websites*), allow you to:

- pause videos and add assessment questions
- annotate videos, by adding text or images
- integrate polls and surveys
- track student progress and performance via a virtual learning environment (see Chapter 7).

**Try this**     **A day in my life**

Get students to take videos of moments in their daily life and ask them to describe the videos in a presentation. These videos could be of places they visit on a daily basis, for example the bus station, the school canteen, or a local shop. Weaker students can simply describe these locations, while stronger students can collect videos of interactions or activities and describe what's going on in the presentation. This makes the learning personal and immediate.

**✓ Getting it right**    **Less is more**

Keep things simple: less is more in online design. Be conservative in using features. Too much clutter will weaken your message. Don't ignore the power of text to switch topic or highlight a point in a video lesson. Finally, give careful consideration to the video you are using. Ask yourself: if the video was to stand on its own, would its message be clear?

**Why this works** ⇒    **Working with video**

Studies have shown that learning with video helps increase engagement and support knowledge retention. Video offers opportunities to explain concepts that would be difficult to convey in any other way. The combination of vision, sound, movement, and text can appeal to students with varying learning preferences, all within the context of one individual unit of content.

# 6      Social networks

## What are social networks?

Social networks are websites or apps that allow its users to share and exchange their interests, ideas, experiences, and information. Some smaller social networks focus on specific topic areas, (such as Football Fanatix for lovers of football and Foodie for baking enthusiasts), but most of the larger networks (such as Instagram and Facebook), have created a space for self-expression which is not bound by specific topics or interests. Within the larger networks, smaller 'interest groups' emerge as members make 'friends' who, in turn, have friends, each one with their own set of interests and sub-networks.

## Security online

Social networks can be used in countless ways to positive effect in teaching and learning. However, there are risks inherent in sharing and collaborating online which go beyond viruses and identity theft (see Chapter 2). When you and your students join a social network, you establish an online identity. As you link to 'friends' who, in turn, have friends, and friends of friends, your information can travel around the world.

If you educate yourself and your students on internet safety, you can limit any risk and have an enriching experience. Below are some key points to consider.

- Get students to sign an internet code of conduct. Many internet safety groups, such as BECTA (see *Useful websites*) in the UK, have sample documents you can use. Another internet safety group to consider is i-SAFE (see *Useful websites*), a non-profit group in the USA.
- Explore the structure of the social network you are considering using. Can you adjust privacy settings? Nowadays, most major social networks have privacy settings which can allow you to control who can have access to your information. Be sure to check that your students have set their profiles to 'private'. Wisely, many social networks are now setting profile defaults to 'private'.
- Even if you control access to your network, only post information you are comfortable showing to other people. Remember that, once something is posted publicly online, you cannot make it private. Even if you delete the information, it could still be sitting locally on someone's computer. Make sure your students understand this.

- Don't share passwords and, when creating passwords, take care to make them 'strong'. Strong passwords are complex and difficult for hackers to break (to check the strength of your password, see *Useful websites*). Some tips for creating strong passwords are to:
  - make your password long
  - mix numbers, letters, and special characters
  - substitute symbols or numbers for letters (e.g. 'ye$' for 'yes', '!ndia' for 'India', and so on)
  - use a word or phrase that only you can understand.
- Create usernames that do not hint at your real identity.
- Consider using a new email account to set up your online account. That way, if your information is compromised, your personal email account is still protected.
- If you are working on social networks in a public domain (e.g. in a school computer lab), make sure you and your students always log out after a session.
- Using large, open social networks also presents the risk of students accessing inappropriate content. Most social networking sites do not allow children under 13 years of age to create profiles, so this should be the minimum age limit for students to join social networks as well.

## Using social networks in EFL teaching

Social networks provide rich opportunities to use English in a targeted, purposeful way. In fact, each step in the process of using the network creates multiple opportunities for authentic communication. Below are two steps common to most social networks.

1 **Create a profile:** All social networking sites will require a new user to create a profile, asking for some personal information (such as name, email address, etc.).

2 **Find friends:** Once you have created a profile, the next logical step is to look for 'friends'. Friends can be people you already know or those with whom you share similar interests. In many cases, the social network will make recommendations based on interests, location, or friends you already have. It is important to evaluate potential friends carefully when working on open social networks. Even closed networks with more oversight and scrutiny of members cannot guarantee complete safety. Note: you will not be able to correspond directly with a prospective friend until they agree to join your network.

You can use the IWB to show your students how you are creating your profile, then ask them to create theirs and to join your network.

## Image-sharing networks

Some social networks are image-based and allow you to post and share photographs, videos, and animation free of charge. One such network is Flickr, which is an easily searchable database of images where each picture is tagged with searchable keywords (see Screenshot 6.1). For Flickr and more image-sharing networks, see *Useful websites*.

SCREENSHOT 6.1    *Flickr*

The advantage of image-sharing networks is that they enable you to create folders of images for your students to work with at their own computer, or for the class to use together on the IWB. Using an image-sharing network will save you hours of time searching for appropriate images and also save you money on copying and other reproduction costs. These image-sharing networks function in much the same way as other social networks: you create a profile, find friends, and join groups.

Organizing pictures on Flickr is quick and straightforward. Before you start, organize the files on your computer into easy-to-identify folders. After you log on to Flickr and click on the 'upload images' button on the home page, select 'choose photos', then locate and click on the photos you would like to upload. Remember, holding down the left button of your mouse will allow you to select multiple images. At this point, a list of your selected photos will appear on the Flickr website. You can set your privacy level so that only you and your friends can access the photos before clicking 'upload'. You then have a further option to state whether you want your gallery to be accessible to online searches or not. You can now add tags and descriptions to your photos and add them to existing sets (galleries), or create and add them to a new gallery. If you are in a hurry, you can always edit and organize your photos later. Simply click on 'organize' and choose what you want to work on.

**Try this** ☞   **Guess where/what**

Use images to practise the language of opinion and speculation (*I think it's
..., It must be ..., It can't be ...*). Select images (or upload your own photos to the
website and/or an image-sharing network for the class) and have students
guess where the image was taken and/or what the image shows. This is a
particularly fun activity for students to do as group or pair work.

**Try this** ☞   **Photo exchange**

Use the 'closed-group' function on Flickr (or another image-sharing network;
see *Useful websites*) to safely share photos and commentary with another class
in your school, or a twinned school with which you already have links.

**Try this** ☞   **Create a photo story**

Upload your images to your Flickr account. Click on the 'set' button and select
images to form a story. Under each picture, get students to write text for the
story. Classmates can correct or make suggestions by using the 'comments'
function that comes with each picture.

# Part 3 Putting it into practice

# 7 Virtual learning environments and social learning platforms

## Basic VLE functionality

**Virtual learning environments (VLEs)**, also known as learning management systems, are software platforms with tools and resources that allow teachers and institutions to track, deliver, and report on online learning. Some VLEs are **open source**, meaning they are free to use, while others such as Blackboard (see *Useful websites*) charge a fee per user. It must be noted, however, that open source VLEs are not simple to set up and probably require expert support to configure. This support and maintenance should be taken into account when weighing the costs and benefits of a particular VLE. VLEs are not solutions for individual teachers. Opting for a VLE needs to take place at an institutional level. Implementing the VLE will take a lot of planning and coordination and will not take place overnight. As we saw in Chapter 1 (see 'Institutional technology plans' on page 16), technical support will be a crucial component of a successful VLE implementation. VLEs come in many shapes and sizes, with quite sophisticated tools. The basic tools that almost all VLEs share are outlined below.

- **Course management tools.** These give users the ability to:
  - create courses and syllabuses
  - manage lists of students
  - generate calendars, reminders, and alerts
  - upload and manage multiple forms of media (documents, presentations, audio, video, and images) to the course for students to access.
- **Collaboration and engagement tools.** Examples of these include email integration, chats, discussion forums, blogs, and wikis.
- **Assessment tools:** The ability to create quizzes and tests using a variety of item types, such as multiple choice, gap-fill, sequencing, and drag and drop.
- **Gradebook and reporting tools.** These tools give teachers the ability to track student and class progress by assigning and reviewing grades at exercise and course level. Teachers can also export these grades if required.

In addition to the core functionalities outlined above, most new generation VLEs also offer the following tools.

- **Synchronous communication tools.** Examples of these include instant messaging and videoconferencing, as well as newsfeeds.
- **Detailed analytics.** Quantitative data on learning and assessment: from time on task and participation to results of assessments; from individual students to an entire school; and from an individual question all the way up to the sum of all tests.
- **Basic gamification and rewards systems.** Examples of these include points, badges, and leadership boards (see Chapter 11).

## Potential drawbacks of VLEs

VLEs have traditionally been designed with an 'instructor' focus, i.e. with an eye to helping teachers build courses and organize content consistently and efficiently. While it certainly is possible to ask students to dip in and out of content in the order they choose, the linear structure of most VLEs, which are typically navigated via a vertical and horizontal menu bar, reinforces a linear progression through content (see Screenshot 7.1).

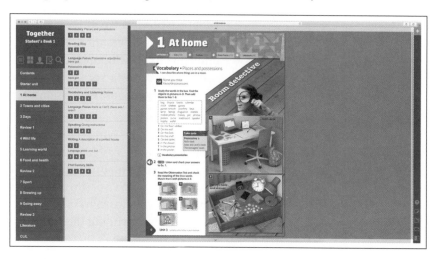

SCREENSHOT 7.1    *Virtual learning environment (VLE)*

Content in the VLE has traditionally been created using simple authoring tools which allow teachers to add text, media, and hyperlinks. While this makes it simple to create relatively straightforward, mainly text-driven content, it has one big drawback – you cannot take the courses with you. They are anchored to the VLE tools.

With the growth of social learning, VLEs have been criticized for not being learner-centred. Critics say that VLEs are tools to control learning, rather than instruments aimed at empowering students to manage their own education. While there is some truth in this, it is indisputable that VLEs can simplify the lives of teachers and students, and provide access to learning at any time of day or night. Ultimately, it is the tasks that teachers set which will determine how learner-centred the course is, not the platform on which it is delivered.

## Social learning platforms

Over recent years, new approaches have emerged that challenge the rather uninspiring design of VLEs and the locked-down approach to learning. These new approaches reflect a fundamental change in thinking about the design and delivery of educational content. Instead of clearly defined activities and resources organized in a set progression and alignment, next-generation VLEs will be based on a building block approach, where users can add and subtract resources and configure functionality to meet personal needs. These features will be accessed through online marketplaces, similar to app stores, which will allow students to select and organize resources to meet their needs. Systems will be 'open', as opposed to being constrained to a particular VLE, and will meet universal design standards. This will allow for content created elsewhere to be easily imported into a VLE, and for local content to be exported without complications, allowing for any content to integrate, regardless of its origin.

Since the first edition of this book, social learning has become a key element of most learning tools. Wikispaces, for example, has gone from being a wiki-creation tool to a 'social writing platform' (see *Useful websites*). In addition to wiki creation, Wikispaces now provides classroom-management functionality, including tools for tracking student activity in real time, creating groups and projects, and interacting with peers in much the same way as on Facebook, with a familiar newsfeed.

One of the most popular social learning websites is Edmodo (see Screenshot 7.2). With a look and feel very close to Facebook, Edmodo allows you to manage classes, create assignments, track progress, award badges, and share content. But what makes it especially interesting is the ability to add apps to the website to enhance the functionality. This allows you to customize your learning environment according to the needs of yourself and your students, without the need for a more elaborate VLE.

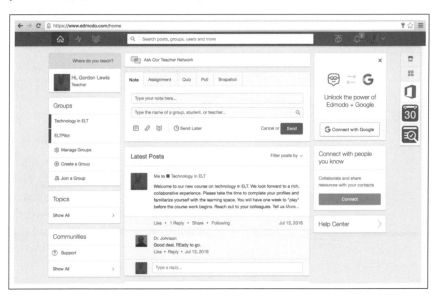

SCREENSHOT 7.2    *Edmodo*

# 8 Learning technology and assessment

There is no area of education where technology is having more impact than in assessment. However, this impact is also highly controversial. Teachers and parents/carers regret class time lost to 'teaching to the test' and fear that high-stakes, standardized exams threaten teacher autonomy and the ability to address learner needs. While this may be true, the issue is less about the assessments themselves and more about how they are used. Technology has given us access to incredible amounts of data on learning which, when used formatively, gives us valuable insight into student and teacher performance. However, data-driven solutions cannot be the only measure of success and should not override or threaten the role of the teacher but rather provide support. While certainly valuable in providing insights into learning, the risk of this type of data collection is that it will be the primary driver of education and generate troubling washback (how tests affect the classroom teaching that leads up to them) into curricula and teaching decisions.

Today, teachers can create diverse and appealing assessments with the click of a mouse, grade them automatically, and track progress from the individual learner to the class, school, regional level, or even global level. The ability to drill down to the individual learning outcome and roll back up to a comprehensive view of student performance is changing how we view our students. Digital technology for assessment is a powerful tool and must be handled with care. As discussed in Part 1, it is best to first consider your own philosophy of assessment and then select the tools that best help you implement it.

## Types of assessment

For the purposes of this book, we can divide assessment into the following distinct areas.
- **Diagnostic:** Diagnostic assessments, such as placement and progress tests, help teachers understand a student's language level.
- **Summative:** Summative assessments, such as exit tests, focus on learning outcomes and measure learning against established targets.
- **Formative:** Formative assessments are more focused on the learning process than learning outcomes alone, and aim to improve teaching and learning. Some examples are e-portfolios, graphic organizers, peer assessments, and project work.

## Summative assessments

Whatever your position on assessment may be, for most teachers and students, tests and quizzes are a fact of life. Schools, parents/carers, employers and other stakeholders legitimately look for standard measures of student achievement, which are still generally expressed in summative assessments. Creating and grading these has often been a very time-consuming task for teachers, taking away time to focus on learning and give learner-oriented feedback and evaluation. By automating the test creation and grading process, digital technology saves teachers hours of planning time. This alone is a strong reason to integrate digital assessment into your teaching.

## Creating assessments

The value of discrete item testing (which measures knowledge of individual items) versus alternative assessment types can be disputed, but one thing is clear: schools, universities, and other institutions will continue to demand quantifiable results for their students.

The internet offers a wide range of free test-creation tools. Most test generators share a common core set of item types to choose from. The most frequent options are quite familiar to students and teachers:
- multiple choice
- matching
- ordering
- scrambled sentence
- multiple answer
- gap fill
- true/false
- short essay.

There is a lot of variety to be found within these item types. Some test generators also allow you to add images, audio files, and even video. Many also allow you to 'randomize' questions – to shuffle the order or replace questions with others of a similar type. This helps to prevent cheating and allows you to retest students without using the same questions. You can print out the test and deliver it in paper format, or have your students answer the questions online, in which case the computer will generate an automatic score (unless there is an open question, such as a short answer). Screenshot 8.1 shows an example of a test generator in 'edit' mode.

If you don't want to create your own tests, there are a variety of existing options available on the web, some of which are free. Check these tests closely if using them for high-stakes assessment which can have a major impact on a student's future.

SCREENSHOT 8.1    *Free online test generator*

Many publishers offer test generators as supplements to their coursebooks, and these are increasingly being offered exclusively online. Unlike the stand-alone test generators or VLE assessment tools, most publisher test generators are already loaded with items that you can select and arrange according to your needs (see Screenshot 8.2).

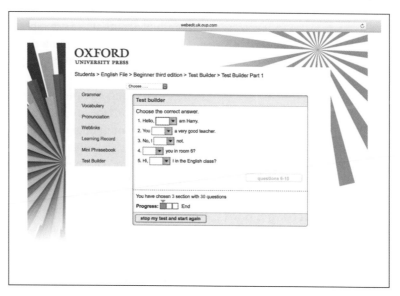

SCREENSHOT 8.2    *Test generator with pre-loaded items*

## Dealing with online tests

There are a number of issues to consider when using online tests. See the following for a description of the most common issues.

### 1  Familiarization

Make sure your students are familiar and comfortable with the testing platform. Taking tests online may be new to them, and each platform has its own design. Let students take a practice test. Show them how to navigate through the test and introduce them to the types of questions they will encounter.

### 2  Bandwidth

If you are planning on testing speaking skills or using multimedia prompts in your assessments, be aware that both of these require strong bandwidth to run smoothly. Digital data, particularly video data, require considerable bandwidth to run smoothly. Conduct bandwidth testing prior to launching an assessment and remember that the more users there are using bandwidth at any given time, the slower the connection will be. So testing 30 students at once will be very different to testing them individually at allotted times.

### 3  Settings

Testing online may require you to adjust settings on your school devices or students' devices. Familiarize yourself with the platform requirements and set up your school computers, or get your students to set up their own devices, accordingly. Typical considerations are:
- choice of browser and version required
- firewalls (which might block your content)
- installation of additional software (such as Flash, Java, and so on).

### 4  Cheating

There is no foolproof way to prevent cheating if you are administering an assessment at a distance. For long-distance students (those who complete their course entirely online), this can pose a serious problem to an institution. In some cases, institutions require all long-distance students to sit their final exams at the same physical location. Other institutions require each student to sign an 'honour code', a set of rules which they agree to follow. There are also technology solutions to help. Some of these solutions monitor the student environment via webcams, while others remotely monitor a student's computer screen, noting where the student clicks. Other applications focus on the authentication of test takers by requesting documentation or information to prove identity. This is necessary because, if you have never actually met a long-distance student, you need to find a way of confirming whether the person who is logged on is really the student registered for the course.

 *Getting it right*

**Item types**

With the exception of gap-fill and short essay questions, many of these item types require students to 'drag and drop' their answer choices into appropriate spaces on a screen. Note that this function works differently on computers compared to tablets or smartphones. Consult your device manual to check how this works.

## Grading

With the exception of open questions, such as short essays, the moment your student submits a test for grading, the questions are automatically scored. This saves a huge amount of time.

If your institution works with a VLE, test creation tools will be integrated into the platform and students' results will automatically be added to a gradebook, where you can track progress on individual tests and across an entire course (see Screenshot 8.3). If you don't work with a VLE, you will need to manually enter the results from a test generator into your school grading system. Gradebooks allow you to analyze student performance from an individual item through an entire school career.

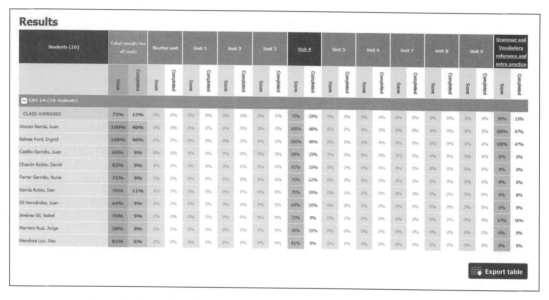

### Results

| Students (20) | Total results for all units Score | Completed | Starter unit Score | Completed | Unit 1 Score | Completed | Unit 2 Score | Completed | Unit 3 Score | Completed | Unit 4 Score | Completed | Unit 5 Score | Completed | Unit 6 Score | Completed | Unit 7 Score | Completed | Unit 8 Score | Completed | Unit 9 Score | Completed | Grammar and Vocabulary reference and extra practice Score | Completed |
|---|---|---|---|---|---|---|---|---|---|---|---|---|---|---|---|---|---|---|---|---|---|---|---|---|
| **ESO 1A (10 students)** | | | | | | | | | | | | | | | | | | | | | | | | |
| CLASS AVERAGES | 75% | 15% | 0% | 0% | 0% | 0% | 0% | 0% | 0% | 0% | 75% | 20% | 0% | 0% | 0% | 0% | 0% | 0% | 0% | 0% | 0% | 0% | 54% | 13% |
| Alonso García, Juan | 100% | 40% | 0% | 0% | 0% | 0% | 0% | 0% | 0% | 0% | 100% | 48% | 0% | 0% | 0% | 0% | 0% | 0% | 0% | 0% | 0% | 0% | 100% | 47% |
| Balmes Font, Ingrid | 100% | 40% | 0% | 0% | 0% | 0% | 0% | 0% | 0% | 0% | 100% | 48% | 0% | 0% | 0% | 0% | 0% | 0% | 0% | 0% | 0% | 0% | 100% | 47% |
| Castillo Garrido, Juan | 69% | 9% | 0% | 0% | 0% | 0% | 0% | 0% | 0% | 0% | 69% | 15% | 0% | 0% | 0% | 0% | 0% | 0% | 0% | 0% | 0% | 0% | 0% | 0% |
| Chacón Rubio, David | 82% | 9% | 0% | 0% | 0% | 0% | 0% | 0% | 0% | 0% | 82% | 15% | 0% | 0% | 0% | 0% | 0% | 0% | 0% | 0% | 0% | 0% | 0% | 0% |
| Ferrer Garrido, Nuria | 71% | 9% | 0% | 0% | 0% | 0% | 0% | 0% | 0% | 0% | 71% | 12% | 0% | 0% | 0% | 0% | 0% | 0% | 0% | 0% | 0% | 0% | 0% | 8% |
| García Rubio, Dan | 70% | 11% | 0% | 0% | 0% | 0% | 0% | 0% | 0% | 0% | 70% | 15% | 0% | 0% | 0% | 0% | 0% | 0% | 0% | 0% | 0% | 0% | 0% | 8% |
| Gil Hernández, Juan | 64% | 9% | 0% | 0% | 0% | 0% | 0% | 0% | 0% | 0% | 64% | 15% | 0% | 0% | 0% | 0% | 0% | 0% | 0% | 0% | 0% | 0% | 0% | 0% |
| Jiménez Gil, Isabel | 70% | 9% | 0% | 0% | 0% | 0% | 0% | 0% | 0% | 0% | 72% | 9% | 0% | 0% | 0% | 0% | 0% | 0% | 0% | 0% | 0% | 0% | 67% | 16% |
| Marrero Ruiz, Jorge | 38% | 9% | 0% | 0% | 0% | 0% | 0% | 0% | 0% | 0% | 38% | 15% | 0% | 0% | 0% | 0% | 0% | 0% | 0% | 0% | 0% | 0% | 0% | 0% |
| Mendoza Luz, Alex | 81% | 6% | 0% | 0% | 0% | 0% | 0% | 0% | 0% | 0% | 81% | 9% | 0% | 0% | 0% | 0% | 0% | 0% | 0% | 0% | 0% | 0% | 0% | 0% |

Export table

SCREENSHOT 8.3    *VLE gradebook*

Many gradebooks display data on an easy to understand graphic interface, often called a 'dashboard'. This allows you to quickly get a snapshot of student learning and identify trends. For example, if the gradebook shows you that a majority of students are not getting a question about the present perfect correct, you can focus your teaching appropriately. If tests and gradebooks are used as snapshots of learning, they can have a distinct formative value for the classroom (see Chapter 9).

## Evaluating speaking and writing

While learning technology has proven itself very effective in assessing listening and reading skills, evaluating speaking and writing skills has been more difficult. As such, human graders continue to be the norm in language teaching, and this will not change radically in the near future. While current learning technology is effective in measuring discrete aspects of speaking and writing, it struggles to measure communication. Critics point to the fact that by breaking down the assessment of speaking and writing into discrete items, rather than allowing for a holistic evaluation, current automated assessment encourages teachers to take a fragmented, 'teaching to the test' approach when preparing students for the tests instead of promoting authentic communication.

Nevertheless, technology is advancing. With the capacity to handle huge amounts of data, the ability of digital tools to process natural language is making it possible to automatically evaluate more than just grammar, vocabulary, and, in the case of speaking, pronunciation. The technology is not perfect yet, and human validation may still be required, but if used wisely, the automated assessment tools could help teachers identify the highest and lowest samples, allowing them to dig deeper into the evaluation of the less clear-cut responses.

For the current context, we need not take an either/or approach. Automated assessment of speaking and writing skills can complement teacher evaluation and remove some of the subjectivity. It can also make teachers aware of aspects of performance (pronunciation in speaking, grammar and syntax in writing) they may miss or take longer to grade.

One great advantage of technology is the ability to deliver speaking assessments without the need to have all of the students in the same classroom simultaneously. Many testing programs allow audio recording: students can speak into their computer, tablet, or smartphone and upload the audio file for evaluation. Students can give presentations or perform a specific speaking task such as describing a friend or explaining a process. In integrated skills tasks, students might listen to someone speaking on a subject, read a short article about the same topic and then answer questions, verbally or written, which require input from both sources.

The above examples are not really communicative. There is no real interaction. To evaluate communicative competence, videoconferencing software (such as Skype, WebEx, Adobe Connect, and Zoom) allows students to interact in real time with the teacher (interview format) or communicate with other students, either together in one location or across the world. The sessions can be evaluated in real time or can be recorded and then evaluated later. While not quite the same as sitting together in a physical space, videoconferencing technology is about as close to face-to-face communication as you can get.

## Formative assessment

Any activity involving student production can ultimately contribute to formative assessment. What makes learning technology so compelling in this regard is the sheer diversity of options available for students to demonstrate their abilities, and the motivation this can give to be creative and take chances with language.

### Instant engagement

One particularly exciting development is the growth of instant engagement systems in classrooms. These are wireless systems that allow students to respond to teacher questions via a 'clicker' (a handheld response system not unlike a TV remote control) or by using their own networked devices (see 'Integration models' on page 86). The answers are then projected onto a large screen so that students can see the responses in real time.

Based on the principle of polling, instant engagement systems such as Socrative (see Screenshot 8.4) increase motivation and engagement, as well as provide valuable information for formative assessment. In this case, the assessment is diagnostic at whole-class level. Teachers can ask content questions to test for knowledge or simply gauge student interest, all in real time. Consider a typical situation: you are teaching a concept and conduct a basic concept check with individual students and ask if there are any questions. In a class of 30, you may elicit answers from four or five students. With instant engagement systems, you can engage the entire class with minimal effort or preparation and see whole-class results and individual scores instantaneously, modifying your instruction accordingly. Results are anonymous, allowing shy students to express themselves in a safe environment. Instant engagement systems can also be a lot of fun, as questions can be used to build games, encouraging healthy competition (see *Useful websites*).

SCREENSHOT 8.4 *Socrative*

## E-portfolios

E-portfolios are examples of student work, documenting student learning over time. E-portfolio assessment is one of the most popular forms of alternative assessment in the language classroom, at least in principle. In real life, physical portfolio assessment has followed a much more difficult road to acceptance. Teachers and students often complain about the size of physical portfolios and the awkwardness of handling and storing them. As a result, they have been implemented haphazardly, with varying degrees of depth, intensity, and success.

E-portfolios offer a far less complicated and more easily managed alternative. Rather than storing reams of paper, e-portfolios are electronic files hosted on a website, stored locally on a personal device, or on an external hard drive/USB.

## European Language Portfolio

The European Language Portfolio (ELP) is perhaps the most widely used and well-known e-portfolio assessment tool in the language-teaching world. With its introduction, keeping a language learning e-portfolio has been 'officially sanctioned' and has become, again at least in principle, an official document with the validity of a test or exam.

This e-portfolio, which is approved by the Council of Europe, is broken down into three key sections:

- language passport (listing official transcripts, exam qualifications)
- language biography (which includes learning goals, can-do statements, and self-assessment)
- dossier (a body of work reflecting student learning and achievement).

There have been numerous projects to develop digital versions of this e-portfolio. Most of these versions are available for free (see *Useful websites*).

## Creating your own e-portfolio

Many teachers prefer to create their own e-portfolios rather than use a template such as the ELP discussed above. If you choose this route, it is worth considering the following steps.

1  **Define the purpose of the e-portfolio:** The first thing you need to do is define the purpose. There are two basic types of e-portfolio: working e-portfolios (demonstrating work in progress and focusing on reflection); and presentation e-portfolios (showing examples of completed work and aimed at demonstrating ability or competence in a particular area). Think about who will see the e-portfolios. Perhaps the students will show them to their parents/carers. Will the e-portfolio be part of a final grade?

2  **Organize the e-portfolio:** How do you want to segment the e-portfolio? Will you divide the work up by topic area? Perhaps you want the work to be related to a particular skill or 'can-do' statement?

3  **Choose the appropriate technology:** E-portfolios can be created with any number of technology tools, from word processing to PowerPoint, wikis, blogs, note-sharing websites (such as Evernote), or the ever-expanding set of Google tools. Your decision will necessarily be influenced by your local situation (if internet access is difficult, do not choose wikis or blogs; if your school works with Google Apps for Education, you probably want to stay within that ecosystem) and the personal preferences and skills you and your students bring to the classroom.

4  **Create a folder (locally or in the cloud) with all examples of work:** Rather than adding a piece of work to each individual page of a e-portfolio, it makes more sense to create an archive of all work. You can then link from an e-portfolio page to the relevant part of the archive or, if you wish to display (or embed) the work, you can simply upload selected files from the archive location.

**✓ Getting it right**

**Back up project work**

Backing up your work requires little effort but can make a big difference when you are working on a long-term project such as an e-portfolio. If you don't have a cloud-based storage system, back up all student work on an external hard drive as well as on your computer. You always want to have multiple save locations to be absolutely sure you won't lose your work!

## E-portfolios using a wiki

A wiki is a very useful tool for creating e-portfolios. Because of its editing function, it is easier to manipulate and change than, for example, a blog. As discussed in Chapter 5, the 'history' function automatically allows viewers to trace progress over time rather than simply displaying only the final product. Thus you can have a working e-portfolio showing drafts, and a presentation e-portfolio with a final product, all in the same wiki. The flexibility of hyperlinking allows students to be creative in designing their e-portfolio wiki. Students can create a series of introductory pages to form a core navigational structure for their e-portfolio and add content directly onto a page or link it to examples of work stored elsewhere. Using a wiki e-portfolio, your students can each work on their own version of an e-portfolio document that you have uploaded. The interactivity of the wiki also makes an e-portfolio a far more dynamic document.

## E-portfolios using Evernote

Evernote is a versatile note-taking tool which allows you to write notes, record audio, and upload almost anything. The content is organized into notebooks, which is perfect for e-portfolios, and can also be tagged for easy searching. Evernote also works on multiple devices, so you can work on a smartphone and then switch to a laptop and continue your work with everything saved in the same place.

## Voicethread as an e-portfolio tool

Voicethread is a free online presentation tool which allows students to combine images with commentary in the form of text or audio. It is easy to use and, since it is based online, does not require any downloads to work. Voicethread is also very flexible; it allows users to upload images, videos, and text from a local computer or social networks, such as Flickr or YouTube. These images then become pages in a Voicethread presentation. The student can then write and attach comments to each page. In turn, other students can view and add additional comments to the presentation, making it an interactive experience. The student who created the presentation can delete comments, as they retain control of the presentation.

One great innovation of Voicethread is the possibility it provides to post comments via webcam, audio, or typed-in text. This is a particularly useful tool to help students practise their speaking skills. The commentary function allows learners to engage in a digital conversation anchored by the image presentation. Since the discussion is asynchronous, students have time to reflect and develop their responses – an important factor for language learners.

# 9       Blended learning

## What is blended learning?

**Blended learning** is a blanket term that is widely used but hard to pin down. Like other terms in language teaching, such as communicative language teaching and task-based learning, blended learning can have a narrow definition or capture a wide range of approaches. Taken in its most general sense, blended learning is understood as the integration of technology and classroom instruction. The Online Learning Consortium, a leading organization in the field of blended learning defines the term as courses that 'integrate online with traditional face-to-face class activities in a planned, pedagogically valuable manner'. This definition leaves a lot of room for interpretation. For example, describing something as 'pedagogically valuable' is quite subjective. And while blended learning can support a traditional approach to education, it also has the potential to change an existing model and transform learning.

## Blended learning continuum

Rather than trying to pin down a specific definition of blended learning, it is probably more useful to think of it in terms of a continuum, starting conservatively and moving through models of student and teacher maturity to reach a truly transformational model, as shown in Table 9.1.

| Model 1 | Model 2 | Model 3 | Model 4 |
|---|---|---|---|
| Basic online supplements | Book and online practice with LMS | Basic blended | Flipped classroom |
| **Supplementary** | **Integrated** | **Replacement** | **Transformational** |
| • Companion website<br>• PDFs (worksheets, readings)<br>• Podcasts, videos | • Practice moves online | • Online also replaces some classroom instruction | • Role of teacher and students change<br>• Learner autonomy |

TABLE 9.1    *Blended learning continuum*

Looking at the models in more detail, it is important to note the following.

### Supplementary materials

Supplementary materials extend the classroom by providing additional input and practice that students can work on in their own time, before or after class. These materials can include physical objects (such as videos, audio CDs, DVDs) or computer programs. These are traditionally found in computer labs but are giving way to online options that do not require downloads or peripheral hardware devices, and which are accessible in computer labs or on demand. These supplements can be assigned for homework or self-study and do not tend to be graded by teachers. In this model, the technology is an add-on and does not necessarily change the classroom routine or structure of the course. The tools can, of course, be used in the face-to-face classroom if desired, in order to highlight certain aspects of tasks that students might have done alone online, for example.

### Integrated practice

Integrating digital resources into the learning process takes technology a step further. Here, the technology is often delivered via a VLE (see Chapter 7), meaning that student progress can be monitored by anyone with a password to the system, such as teachers, students, administrators, and parents/carers. Online workbooks are good examples of this kind of tool. Integrated practice tools can have very positive impacts; for the teacher, they significantly reduce marking time. Time-consuming grading of exercises is conducted automatically and results can be displayed graphically via dashboards and charts, making it easy for students and teachers to get a snapshot of learning. Unlike the supplementary materials model, integrated practice does have the potential to change class dynamics. By automating the second 'P' in the PPP (presentation–practice–production) model, it can be moved outside the classroom, either reducing face-to-face hours or freeing up class time for other activities.

### Flipped classroom models

As the name suggests, **flipped classroom** models turn an existing model on its head, with profound implications for teachers and students. In these models, students access content and concepts outside the classroom through multiple web-based media. Unlike the integrated practice model, where only one 'P' (practice) is delivered online, elements of 'presentation' move online as well, freeing up even more time for students to maximize production in the face-to-face environment.

In many ways, flipped classroom models are a reflection of long-standing efforts to promote learner autonomy, changing the power relationship in the classroom. Rather than focusing on providing knowledge, the teacher becomes a facilitator, guiding the student on their path of discovery. Task-based and enquiry-based learning form the basis of this process but, with the power of learning technology, students can access anything at any time, including lectures from respected, engaging professors from around the world.

This shift in the student–teacher relationship is not automatic and needs to be well planned and matched to the digital and academic maturity of the students and teachers. Everyone involved needs to understand and embrace the rationale for transformation.

 **Getting it right**

**Face-to-face classroom**

Don't assume that all students will fully comprehend content only by accessing it online, even if the online assessments that accompany the content show evidence of learning. In many cases, students may just randomly click on answers (known as 'zombie-clicking'), especially if the online activities are not graded, and may even share answers with their peers. Online gradebooks can provide valuable information on learner progress, but they may require further validation in class. Spend some time in class to reconfirm comprehension before moving on to other tasks. Using an instant engagement system (see Chapter 8) is a good way of getting a 'second opinion'.

## Why blended learning?

### Teacher presence

One misconception is assuming that blended approaches can 'replace' the teacher. Whether teaching and learning takes place online or not, the teacher must be present. Research studies have shown that teacher presence is the single most important factor in student motivation online. This is especially true if you are using communicative tools such as blogs, wikis, forums, or even text chats. What makes these tools powerful is the fact that students have an audience. If students post their thoughts and ideas and get no feedback, their motivation will quickly decrease.

Managing interaction and feedback in blended-learning environments requires a shift in teacher work schedules that can be difficult for many schools to accommodate. In order to keep students on track and focused, teachers need to regularly monitor online learning outside the traditional class schedule. Logging in to the system daily for short periods to review what students have been doing will be more effective than doing so in a single long session once a week. It is important for you to demonstrate best practice for your students to follow.

 **Getting it right**

**Be present**

Look out for students who are lagging behind or haven't logged in for a while and give them a 'nudge' by email or text if your system allows. Even if you warn them in advance, students may still be surprised to see that you are 'monitoring' their progress.

If you don't have time to do a full evaluation of an assignment – be it a blog post, collaborative task, or discussion post – send students a brief message acknowledging that you have seen it and will follow up with more feedback. There is nothing more discouraging to students than working hard on a project, only to be met by silence.

 **Getting it right**

**Facilitate conversation**

Encourage peer feedback. As part of their assessment, get students to post comments about what others have written or created. You may also want to get them to peer-edit before submitting a document to you for final evaluation. When working with wikis or other collaborative tools, monitor the feedback and share it with the rest of the class.

## Flipped classroom courses

### Designing flipped classroom courses

Flipped classroom models come in many shapes and sizes and need to fit the realities of the specific context. Here are some points to bear in mind.

#### Finding the blend

What is the desired ratio between online and face-to-face instruction? Will you choose an equal split, or a 75:25% delivery? Consider the amount of support your students will need. A model dedicating 75% to online instruction requires a lot of discipline on the part of your students. The Online Learning Consortium defines blended courses as requiring a minimum of 30% online instruction, but this is by no means set in stone.

#### Chunking the learning

Once you have determined your blend, you will need to divide up the learning across the school year. When will you hold your face-to-face lessons? What will you expect students to have covered between lessons?

#### Develop study plans

While blended models allow students to access content virtually anywhere, at any time, if we do not help them to organize their learning, they will often not be able to keep pace. Many students (and teachers) may have studied in contexts where autonomous learning was not prioritized and so experience difficulties managing their online work. In flipped classroom models, where face-to-face lessons are dependent upon regular student engagement, this can destroy a well-thought-out lesson. Students need to be trained to take control of their learning. Be prescriptive until you feel they have internalized expectations, and give them a study plan that outlines what you expect them to do each day. You can always relax these guidelines later.

#### Synchronous versus asynchronous learning

In blended learning, it is important to consider the balance between not only face-to-face and online instruction but also between synchronous learning (real time) and asynchronous learning (any time). It can be argued that a 100% online course with both elements is as blended as a course with a physical classroom component. There are pros and cons for each model. Synchronous models provide immediate feedback and discussion, which may feel more natural to students. On the other hand, some students may need more time to think and develop ideas, or may be shy and intimidated by other classmates. For these students, asynchronous environments may be more comfortable.

**Why this works** ⫸ 

> **Blended learning**
>
> Blended learning combines the best of online learning, both in class and outside class, with the immediacy of classroom instruction. It allows for substantial differentiation of instruction so that students get more of what they need and less of what a coursebook dictates. It provides flexibility of learning without losing the support that can exist in the physical classroom. When implemented thoughtfully, blended learning promotes autonomy and increases student engagement by giving them motivating content and tools to express themselves in ways most meaningful to them. Blended learning also makes a teacher's life easier by simplifying the management of learning and resources, allowing them to focus on making classroom instruction relevant and motivating.

# 10 Mobile learning

It was estimated that by the end of 2016 more than two billion people worldwide owned a smartphone. Various sources believe that by 2020, this number could grow to six billion. Equally interesting is the fact that more than half of all internet access comes through mobile devices. Smartphones are clearly positioned to be the main hub of all internet activity in the near future.

For these reasons alone, it is important to address the issue of educational uses of mobile technology. By 'mobile technology', we mean smartphones as well as tablets and e-readers. Today, these devices are more powerful than most computers of less than a generation ago; we can use the devices to connect, search, and create on a level comparable to that of a computer. This has major implications for in-class and out-of-class activities.

## Working with smartphones and tablets

Tablets are essentially large versions of smartphones when it comes to their home screens full of apps. Due to the larger size of tablets, however, students can perform many functions that would be difficult to do on a smartphone, such as reading and writing longer documents.

The great strength of tablets is their versatility. Equipped with most of the functionality of both computers and smartphones, they are arguably the most versatile mobile devices, although new smartphones with bigger screens are beginning to blur the distinction. Most tablets offer both wi-fi and mobile connectivity, allowing students to have maximum access even in environments where wi-fi is not available. Generally, working with wireless networks is cheaper than working over a mobile network. Mobile data is tied to telephone plans and can be very expensive if managed poorly. Also, if students are using their own devices, they will be eating into their own personal data plans.

Despite their larger size, tablets are still devices aimed primarily at consuming rather than creating content. Selecting and moving text or objects can be slow and frustrating on a tablet compared to the more precise 'point and click' functionality of a mouse. It is not surprising that tablets have been most successful in primary classrooms, where chunks of text tend to be smaller, and objects on the screen larger and easier to move.

 **Getting it right**

**Battery issues**

Mobile devices are as easy to put away as they are to take out, and have the added advantage of loading much faster than computers, so there is no long wait as students log in. However, you do need to keep device batteries fully charged. Make sure all devices have enough power to get through a lesson.

## Basic functionalities of smartphones and tablets

It is safe to say that the majority of mobile devices allow users to:
- send/receive text messages, email, and instant messaging
- browse the web
- play audio and video
- record audio and video, take photos, and share them instantaneously.

With these functionalities alone, there is a seemingly endless array of creative tasks you can ask students to perform.

**Try this** ☞ **What is it?**

Send students a photo or short video of a location, action, or object. Make sure the stimulus is not entirely obvious. Encourage students to guess what it is. Alternatively, let the students go out and create their own 'mystery' photos and videos. Taking this a step further, create a treasure hunt by sending students photos and videos as clues.

**Try this** ☞ **Expanding the coursebook**

Ask students to take photos or conduct interviews outside of class as a personalized extension of typical coursebook topics, such as family, city, shopping, etc.

 **Getting it right**

**Chunking content**

Students' attention spans on mobile devices are short, so chunk content into small units. Keep texts to a few paragraphs and videos to three minutes maximum. Long texts are difficult to read on a smartphone and free writing can be challenging. Tablets offer more ease of writing and were designed for reading and watching video, making them ideal for these activities. Remember that if you are working over mobile networks as opposed to wi-fi, lengthy videos will eat up lots of data, which can be very expensive.

## Mobile technology and its influence on language

Inevitably, mobile technology and the web have influenced language use. In the past, text messages were limited to a 140 character limit so abbreviations and acronyms were used to fill the message with as much information as possible. This has since extended to other methods of online communication such as email, instant messaging, and social networking due to the 'fast' nature of online communication. **Emoticons** have also developed over the years, from a combination of keyboard characters to small images that can be embedded into texts. For example:

:-) → ☺ (happy)

:-( → ☹ (sad)

This poses a great challenge to teachers and, to some, is corrupting language. Clearly, we want to make language learning relevant to students and, in this sense, the characteristics of digital communication can't be ignored. Below are two activities you can promote language learning and still integrate the characteristics of digital communication into your class.

**Try this** ☞ **Custom emoticons**

Show students examples of common emoticons and text abbreviations (LOL, BTW, etc.) and ask them to tell you what they symbolize/mean. Invite students to share some other emoticons and abbreviations they know. Put the students into small groups and give each group a topic, e.g. holidays. Ask each group to use emoticons and abbreviations to write messages or a short dialogue. The texts can be a mixture of 'normal' writing, emoticons, and abbreviations. Alternatively, ask one group of students to draft questions which other students must answer using emoticons only.

# Apps

Apps are computer programs that you can download to your smartphone or tablet. They offer users simplified touch navigation for programs which otherwise require a keyboard on a home computer. Depending on what kind of operating system your device has, you can find apps in digital marketplaces such as Apple's App Store for iPhones, Google Play for Androids, and the Microsoft Store for Windows. While many apps are free, not all of them are available across all operating platforms. And, while this is becoming less common, it is not guaranteed that an app for an iPhone will be available for an Android.

Nowadays there is an app for almost every aspect of our daily lives, allowing teachers to build authentic tasks. Some common apps that lend themselves to language practice include weather apps, restaurant review apps, travel apps, public transport apps, film apps with trailers of films, and sports apps with league tables.

**Try this** ☞ **Navigation/Map apps**

Use navigation and map apps to get students to calculate distances, times, or describe routes. These routes could be relatively simple like students' journeys to school or more complicated like different ways of travelling between cities in their own or a different country. Language input can vary by task, including giving directions, comparing, measuring, etc. Activating localization service on a smartphone can even allow for navigation activities in real time.

**Try this** ☞ **Currency exchange apps**

These are good for working with numbers, comparatives, and superlatives, and can contribute to cultural awareness. Get students to calculate the price of the last item of food or clothing they bought in three different common currencies.

Then get them to search online to find out if they would have to pay more or less when buying the items in countries using the different currencies. Students can also track currency rates over time, leading to interesting discussions about current events.

**Try this** ☞   **Using dictionaries and thesauruses**

Dictionaries and thesauruses are great reference tools. At a certain point in the lesson, give students a short list of keywords to cross-check in different online dictionaries, with a time limit. Ask them to say which definitions they prefer and why. Later in the lesson or course, ask them to search for synonyms and antonyms of the keywords using an online thesaurus.

## Social network apps

Social network apps, such as Facebook, Instagram, Pinterest, Twitter, Vine, YouTube, and hundreds more, allow you to create open or closed communities to share ideas, content, or tasks. You can keep things personal or communicate with the entire world. Although these apps are also available as desktop programs, nowadays the majority of users update their accounts in real time, as they go about their daily lives. See something interesting? Post it. Feel like saying something? Tweet it or upload a video. It would be intrusive and unrealistic to expect students to share their personal social networks in a classroom setting. Instead, consider building a 'closed' group for your class (i.e. a group that cannot be seen publically). You can use the closed group to communicate with your students, for example messaging out homework, or simply posting interesting ideas, like a word of the day or a challenge for the day.

## QR code apps

QR (quick response) codes are black-and-white square images that store hyperlinks to websites (see Figure 10.1). Essentially, QR code apps use the device's camera to read the QR code and take users to the given web address. The codes are essentially quick and easy links to web pages. There is no need to open a browser and type in a web address. QR codes are standardized worldwide and can easily be created using a QR code generator. Most smartphones have built-in QR code readers, but there are many free apps available to download.

FIGURE 10.1    *QR code*

In addition to QR codes, there are lots of other scanning apps that can enhance or 'augment' reality. These apps can:
- provide information about a product by taking a photograph
- translate a menu or street sign into another language.

**Try this ☞** **QR codes for group projects**

Create a QR code for instructions for a group project. Place the codes around your classroom. Each group moves from code to code and performs the task they scan. Alternatively, create QR codes with steps in a WebQuest; for example, *Who was the tallest man in the world? What is the deepest point of the Pacific Ocean?* Additional QR codes can then take students to a useful website which will help them in the WebQuest.

**Try this ☞** **Using QR codes outside the classroom**

If you are able to let students go outside the classroom, consider posting QR codes in locations around your school or even in the surrounding town. The codes could include questions that students would need to ask people they encounter. Another option would be to collect objects to bring back to the classroom.

**✓ *Getting it right*** **Managing apps**

If you plan to use apps with your students, be sure the ones you choose match your students' devices. Take an inventory of all devices at the beginning of the school year and make a list of apps with the operating systems they run on. Only use apps that run on all operating systems.

**✓ *Getting it right*** **Value of apps**

Remember that anything you want to do with an app in the classroom can probably be done in a more traditional way. Weigh the true value of the time spent using the device. Is it providing an educational advantage or is it simply fun? It is fine to do something just for fun, but weigh this against the learning objective.

## Educational apps

The market for educational apps is large and continually growing. Most desktop programs now have app equivalents which allow you to access content via multiple devices. Many new (and often free) language learning apps have emerged over the past few years which allow students to work on their own and at their own pace, with the systems themselves coaching and recommending. Some employ gamification (see Chapter 11) and crowdsourcing or online fund-raising to produce lessons they claim are learner-centred and driven by an analysis of data on each student's performance in the system. That is, while the student learns, the system learns about the student. Others focus on dynamic content such as video and audio clips.

While app technology continues to innovate and change at breathtaking speed, teaching pedagogy underlying these products is not innovating at the same pace. Grammar translation, drilling, and standard PPP dominate in this language app world. This is not a bad thing in itself, and these types of activities have their place in any classroom; but left to stand on their own, it is fair to question just how much learning can be achieved by a student working alone. Moving beyond these traditional teaching methodologies to embrace a new learning model is perhaps the greatest challenge for the future of language learning platforms.

To address this issue, many new language learning apps have added online tutors to complement their technology, acknowledging the central role of teachers in the learning process. Alongside online language courses, there has been exciting progress in support for specific skills. Speech recognition has made tremendous strides, with intelligent apps allowing students to practise speaking and get immediate feedback, not only on pronunciation but coherence as well. Speech recognition apps such as Dragon and Vlingo calibrate to the learner's native language and their L2 level, providing a high degree of personalization. Vocabulary builders, automated writing tutors, etc., are all providing valuable resources to support the core language classroom.

## Just-in-time learning

Mobile devices are perfect for filling in 'empty' time when commuting, queuing, and so on. In a sense, it is not our devices that are mobile, but ourselves. **Just-in-time learning** recognizes the need for access to learning any place and any time. However, not all content or activities are applicable to a smartphone or tablet. For example, you probably wouldn't want to read a very long piece of text on your phone, or type long blog posts. You might be more willing to read an extended text on a tablet, but you probably wouldn't want to create a presentation using a touchscreen.

The time needed to complete a task is also a factor to consider when using mobile devices, certainly smartphones. Attention span is generally shorter with mobile devices than with computers. This means that content needs to be 'chunked' or organized differently for different devices. **Just-in-time learning** is the teaching method that allows students to focus on these chunks of information as needed, to complete the task at hand.

## In-class use

While the benefits of using mobile technology outside class, as a natural extension of overall approaches to technology integration, are fairly obvious, in-class use of smartphones and tablets is much more controversial. Supporters of the integration of mobile technology in the classroom argue that mobile devices are everywhere anyway and that, instead of trying to ban them from the classroom, we should embrace them and have students use them productively rather than allowing them to become a distraction. Many educators point to the opportunities for informal learning – open-ended tasks that allow students to capture language as it flows in their everyday life, and spontaneous learning not restricted by the classroom context.

 **Getting it right**

**Smartphone etiquette**

Smartphones are potential distractions that can easily be misused in the classroom. If you intend to use them in class, you need to set clear rules. Make it clear that smartphones may only be used for specific tasks. These can include taking pictures of the whiteboard, searching for facts and information, adding to a calendar, or simply taking notes. If the smartphone is being used to email or message friends, remind your students of the rules for use and, if misuse continues, consider confiscating the device until the end of class.

## Integration models

There are two main approaches to integrating mobile technology in the classroom: **Bring your own device (BYOD)** and **1-to-1**. Each approach has its pros and cons, as is outlined below.

### BYOD

As the name suggests, the BYOD approach assumes that all students have mobile devices they can bring to school. However, this is not as much a 'given' as one may think. Even in countries with the highest number of smartphone users, only up to 70% of the total population owns a mobile device. Therefore, it is still unrealistic to assume that everyone in a class will have one. Your school may be willing to provide devices. Even so, students may need to work in pairs or groups, so be aware of group sizes, to ensure all students can see the device, and of any personal information on the device that the owner may not want to share. It must also be noted that not all devices are alike; like apps, they have different operating systems, memory, and functionalities, potentially making it difficult for everybody to do the same thing or access the same information in the same way. None of this precludes bringing mobile devices into class, but activities that rely on particular apps will need some preparation in advance to:

- identify the make, model, and operating system of students' devices
- check that each operating system will allow the students to perform the same task in the same way.

 **Getting it right**

**Setting rules**

Using tablets in the classroom can be distracting, especially as students using their own devices will have access to personal content and games, so it's a good idea to set some ground rules first. To get students' focus, introduce some simple commands such as 'screen down' to prompt them to turn over their tablets with screens facing down.

### 1-to-1

Projects which use a 1-to-1 approach are a fairly expensive alternative to BYOD. In a 1-to-1 project, each student is given a standard device, such as a laptop, tablet, or smartphone, to use in class. The devices are often provided by the institution, or purchased by students before joining the class. The advantage here is that all the students are guaranteed the same access and computing power. The drawback is cost, whether to the school or to the individual students and their parents/carers. Cost also extends to repairing broken devices and replacing them when technology becomes obsolete, which can be very fast nowadays. However, the initial cost can be offset through savings, for example by eliminating costly language labs and complementary infrastructure, since 1-to-1 projects are almost always based on cloud solutions.

## IWB or tablet?

Tablets are a particularly interesting alternative to traditional IWB technology. While an individual tablet might seem expensive, it is a fraction of the cost of an IWB. Additionally, tablets do not have to be 'installed' in classrooms. If you don't need to manage multiple devices or regularly pass control to your students, consider using the 'mirroring' function on your device. This will wirelessly link your tablet to a television or projector, displaying your tablet screen for all to see. Note that although Apple TV, Samsung Allshare, and Google's Chromecast all have mirroring functionality, they do not work with every device. Check which option is compatible with your tablet.

If you are considering a 1-to-1 or BYOD implementation, you probably want to consider using classroom management software, which turns your device into a control centre. You can track all activity on your students' devices, send material to these devices, give control to individual devices, and even lock devices when you want to get students' attention.

Instead of getting students to come to the front of the class to interact with a touchscreen, they can work on their devices using all of the tablet's functionality available to them. This can change the dynamic of a classroom, moving the focus away from the front and the teacher. With classroom management software installed on your tablet, you can teach from anywhere in the classroom and still maintain control.

### Configuring tablets

Like smartphones, tablets are most often used as individual devices, as opposed to group devices. Tablets can be highly personalized, which is a large part of their appeal. This personalization needs to be balanced against the need for structure and consistency when used in class. How you approach this will depend on whether you choose to:

- use one tablet (yours) in the classroom (in this case, you have full control over the configuration of the device)
- have a small number of tablets that students must share (if you want student data to be captured by an app or program, you will need to create multiple profiles on a single device)
- adopt 1-to-1 or BYOD initiatives (in this case, you can centrally configure all the devices with each one having a single profile).

Both Google and Apple offer configuration tools to teachers, but it is something that should probably be done in consultation with your institution's IT team.

✓ *Getting it right*

### Writing on a tablet

If students need to do a reasonable amount of writing or typing on a tablet, they should consider using a keyboard and mouse connected to the tablet via a Bluetooth wireless connection (which can be turned on in the device's 'settings'). You can also make writing easier by suggesting students use a stylus instead of their finger. They can then use programs like Microsoft OneNote or MyScript Memo (available through iTunes) to convert handwriting into word-processed documents or notes.

✓ *Getting it right*

### Matching tablet use to age groups

Consider age in your decision to use tablets. Studies have demonstrated that acceptance of tablets in education decreases as the age of students increases. This will certainly change, however, as primary students who have grown up with tablets move up through the system. For the time being, consider the familiarity of your students with the devices. If you work in a school environment, consult with colleagues to understand the kinds of tasks they are implementing. Remember that tools should match tasks.

**Why this works** ⟫

### Mobile technology

Mobile technology gives access to learning anywhere and at any time, allowing us to be productive by listening to a podcast, watching a short video, or even attending a virtual class. Mobile technology also favours communication and connectivity, as opposed to simple consumption of content. Students become 'prosumers' – both producers and consumers of content. Mobile technology is also very personal. The owner can configure the device, customize and personalize the settings, decide on backgrounds, what apps to download and how to group them. Even the protective cases are a personal statement! The device itself can be used privately, or used to connect to the entire world.

# Part 4          Pushing the boundaries

# 11 Adaptive learning

**Adaptive learning** is really quite a simple concept. At its core, it is the digital expression of what teachers are trained to do: observe student performance and modify instruction to meet individual student needs. As any experienced teacher knows, differentiating instruction is time-consuming, especially when dealing with large classes. As such, we tend to teach to the 'middle' of our class.

Adaptive learning technology promises to change this situation. The ability of computers to process huge amounts of data allows us to analyze student learning quickly and efficiently, at a level of detail that would otherwise be impossible. Rather than simply providing data, adaptive learning technology also aims to interpret performance. This is done through an algorithm – a formula which determines a series of decisions based on 'input' that the system receives. In plain terms, algorithms for language learning seek to emulate the decisions an experienced and informed teacher would make in the classroom.

The market for adaptive learning technology is diverse and growing quickly. Currently, the options fall into the two broad segments of adaptive learning content and adaptive learning assessment, as outlined below.

## Adaptive learning content

Adaptive learning technology present students with dynamic content (e.g. questions of varying difficulty) which changes based on how the students perform on each item. Based on a student's performance on an item, the system will respond and adapt accordingly. For example, it may send the student back to an earlier part of the material or course to refresh a previous concept, make a recommendation for further study, or provide a hint.

In many ways, adaptive learning platforms are similar to tutoring services. That is, when a student struggles with a concept or a topic, they can have a session with a tutor. The tutor will listen and provide the appropriate support and intervention. In adaptive learning technology, the algorithm becomes the tutor.

## Adaptive learning assessment

While traditional tests are generally designed as fixed papers, with a set of questions arranged in a specific order, adaptive learning assessments are based on a pool of questions, each of which represents a level of difficulty. The testing engine selects a question for a student to answer. If the student answers correctly, a more challenging question is selected. If the student gets that question wrong, a slightly less challenging question is delivered. This procedure continues until the system identifies the exact level at which the student is consistently answering questions correctly. This can reduce testing time for individual students because the system is designed to gradually filter out questions which are too challenging or not challenging enough from the assessment process.

## Issues in language learning

Language learning poses challenges to adaptive learning technology. Whereas adaptivity is predictable for subjects like maths and science (with their hard facts and clear right and wrong answers), it is less so for language use, which is more layered and complex. Depending on the language task, we need to consider grammatical structures, register, lexis, and even pronunciation. It comes as no surprise, then, that most adaptive apps in the field of language learning focus on discrete item content, covering vocabulary and, especially, grammar, with clear right or wrong answers.

## Gamification

Increasingly, language learning programs are employing elements of games to increase motivation in both formative and summative assessment contexts, as well as practice environments such as online workbooks available. The popular free platform, Duolingo, is a good example of this kind of gamification approach (see Screenshot 11.1).

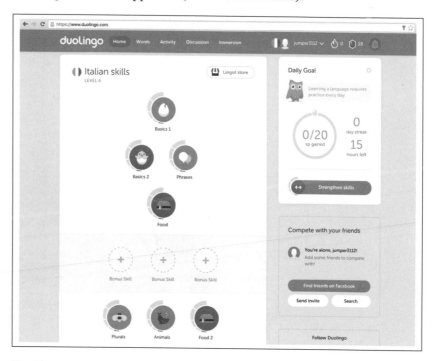

SCREENSHOT II.I  *Duolingo*

Typically, gamification might come in the form of point systems, where students gain points each time they answer a question correctly. Students can compete against each other or simply work on their own to collect points and reach different levels. Point systems can be tied to leader boards showing who has the highest score, locally and potentially across the world. Point systems can be used to automatically award achievement badges, for example when students achieve a certain score in an activity or reach a certain level. Achieving a certain score or level can then have an impact on the rest of the learning or assessment process. For example, if a student achieves a certain level by answering a percentage of questions correctly, new activities will be made available.

It is important to understand that gamification is not the same thing as a game. In games, the learning is contained in the game itself. Gamification, on the other hand, involves adding game elements to non-game contexts. For example, your students might be awarded five points each time they comment on another student's blog. The blog is not a game; it has simply been given a game-like attribute in order to increase motivation. Almost any activity can be gamified, and it is entirely up to the teacher to decide which elements of a classroom activity lead to points; you can assign points to a number of elements or upon completion of the whole activity. Gamified activities do not need to be competitive – you can gamify collaborative tasks. The key is to be consistent in your approach.

Of course, there are numerous language games available online for students and teachers, many with points systems and levels (see Screenshot 11.2). These games can involve anything from simple arcade-style practice, such as shooting down bubbles, to elaborate, multi-player virtual reality games.

SCREENSHOT 11.2     *Online language game*

Gamification also has the potential to support autonomous learning. Students can choose to move faster through content if they feel they are proficient, gaining enough points to move on to a higher level of learning. Gamified platforms with branching systems (e.g. Duolingo), allow students to choose where to start their learning and 'jump over' certain lessons by demonstrating proficiency through a checkpoint quiz. In this way, gamification can contribute to competence-based learning models.

Some educators criticize gamification and claim that incentive systems are superficial and will not maintain students' interest. This is certainly true if gamification is the sole motivator, but when it is employed specifically to make routine tasks more interesting, studies have shown increased engagement from students.

 ***Getting it right***

**Gamification and classroom activities**

Remember that gamified activities do not have to be conducted online. You can award points for in-class participation, project work, and homework assignments. The gamification element simply tracks activity and displays results online.

 ***Getting it right***

**Building a gamification framework**

Gamification takes planning. Make a list of all the activities you intend to award points to and assign values to them. If you are assigning achievement levels, consider how many points a student needs to move up a level. Once you have created this framework, go back to the activities themselves and think about the amount of time required for students to do each one. How does this fit into the reality of your teaching schedule?

## Technology and differentiation

No two students are completely alike; each student brings a unique mix of learning styles to the language classroom. It is a huge challenge for teachers to identify these learning styles and design activities which appeal to the class as a whole, while taking into account the individual needs of each student.

Technology is a powerful tool that you can use to differentiate your classroom instruction and address individual learner needs. For learners who are logical thinkers, tools such as online polls and surveys would be appealing. Those who are visual learners would enjoy working with digital cameras, video, and online resources such as Google Earth. Learners with a strong reflective side will feel comfortable blogging or building up an e-portfolio. Social learners will enjoy instant messaging, email, and social networking. Even physical (kinaesthetic) learners have technology-based options, such as 3D worlds, virtual tours, and animation. The relationship between learning preferences and learning technology can be applied to a specific activity, such as working with a story. You and your students have many options:

- read the story on-screen or print it out
- read the story and listen to an audio recording at the same time

- read a story with accompanying pictures
- read a story with pictures and audio
- watch an animation of the story
- watch a video of the story.

Your class can also create all of the above for an existing story or for a story they compose on their own.

Of course, technology will only have a positive impact on differentiation if the tools available are used selectively. If you send your entire class to a language lab to do the same activity on rows of computers, for example, you will not be appealing to different learning styles. Vary the tasks you assign your students or, within these tasks, vary the roles each student performs. Using technology to diversify instruction requires imagination and planning in its application.

# 12      Looking ahead

One of the biggest challenges for learning technologists is how to accommodate the learner of today while developing the tools for the learners of tomorrow. Our current assumptions could be completely displaced by new innovations within the next three years. Of course, for teachers the focus is on today – on our students and classrooms here and now. Nevertheless, we need to be ready to adapt and become lifelong learners ourselves. We have to accept that permanence simply does not exist any more in our field, and we have to be ready and open to change. While the future may yet take an unexpected turn, here are some predictions that experts believe will impact on learning in the coming years.

## Digital first

Many publishers have struggled to make the jump from print to the digital world. The first steps in this direction have seen the creation of digital 'adaptations' of printed materials, including both supplements and full courses. The coming generation of course materials will flip this model by starting with digital-first course design. In future, printed materials will be supplemental to digital resources, and these will be designed to be used primarily on mobile devices such as smartphones and tablets.

## Intelligent speech recognition and virtual reality

There have been great advances in speech recognition since the days when the technology simply allowed students to compare their own speech to a model. Today, speech recognition can be programmed to recognize a student's native language and provide targeted feedback on pronunciation. What has been lacking is the ability of these technologies to interpret successful oral interaction. Did communication take place? Was the tone appropriate to the context? New natural language processing technology will analyze and monitor what a student says and how he or she interacts with other students or even avatars in virtual worlds. Not only will such technology provide feedback on grammar, vocabulary, and pronunciation; it will also provide feedback on the communication act as a whole, in all its complexity.

## Data and analytics

New learning technology will provide us with more information about our students than ever before. This growth in data will be combined with increasingly intelligent technology to allow us to analyze student performance in more meaningful and holistic ways. It will enable us to anticipate potential problems and provide targeted feedback in the context of real communication – not just evaluating how something was said or written, but also the content of what was communicated.

## The role of the teacher

As a teacher, rest assured, you will not be replaced. Despite all the new advances, the teacher will and should remain at the centre of the teaching process. You will certainly communicate differently with your students, and you may adapt your teaching style over time to fully exploit an online world of limitless information and choice, but the relationship between you and your students will continue to be central to the learning experience. Technology will help you to get the most out of this relationship, but your vision and the empathy you have for your students will be the crucial factor in maintaining their enthusiasm.

Naturally, there are risks associated with learning technology and we need to be vigilant. Above all, we must be sure we understand that purpose drives technology and not vice versa. With this understood, we can have a productive relationship with emerging digital innovations and evaluate and integrate them with confidence.

# Glossary

**1-to-1** Technology implementation initiatives that provide students with their own device.

**Adaptive learning** The use of algorithms to adapt learning and assessment content in accordance with the user's performance on individual items on a given platform.

**Apps** Short for 'Applications'; a self-contained program that performs a specific function (e.g. note-taking apps, media players).

**Asynchronous learning** A teaching method where learning is not constrained by a particular time. Contrasts with *Synchronous learning*.

**Bandwidth** The amount of data or information that can be sent over an internet connection at any one time.

**Blended learning** A teaching approach where learning takes place partly face-to-face in the classroom, and partly online via a computer or mobile device.

**Blog** An online journal that allows users to share content about their interests, ideas, experiences, etc.

**Bookmark** Also known as 'favourite'; a record of a web address stored on a computer's web browser, allowing for quick and easy access to it.

**Bring your own device (BYOD)** Technology implementations where students are permitted to use their own personal mobile devices (laptops, tablets, smartphones) in the classroom.

**Cloud computing** The practice of hosting resources and data on the web, rather than on a personal device, allowing users to access resources and data on any device.

**Communities of practice** Groups of users working collaboratively to achieve a common goal.

**Download** The process by which a file is copied from the web or a shared network to a personal device. Contrasts with *Upload*.

**Emoticon** A small image or combination of keyboard characters used in online communication to express feelings and emotion.

**Firewall** A program that protects a computer from unapproved access by monitoring and filtering data, only allowing safe content to pass.

**Flipped classroom** A teaching approach which overturns the traditional instructional model. Lessons are delivered online for students to view before class, and class time is used for discussions, collaboration, etc.

**Hard drive** A piece of hardware used to store data and software; both built into computers and sold separately for additional memory storage.

**Hyperlink** An electronic link that allows the user to move from one point to another in the same hypertext document or to another document entirely.

**Instant messaging** An online program or app that allows users to communicate in real time.

**Just-in-time learning** A teaching method that allows students to focus on 'chunks' of information as needed, to complete the task at hand.

**Keyword** A word/phrase that captures the main idea of something. It is usually typed into a search engine to find websites relating to the idea/topic. See *Search engine* and *Tagging*.

**MP3** A file format that is used to compress audio.

**MP4** A file format that is used to compress multimedia items such as audio and video; contrasts with *MP3*, which is an older file format for audio only.

**Network** A group of computers that are linked together and can exchange information. Networks can be small-scale (e.g. company intranets) or worldwide (e.g. the internet).

**Open source** Software that is free to use, modify, and redistribute.

**Operating system** Built-in system software that performs all of the essential functions necessary for the device to operate (e.g. running programs, managing memory).

**Personal learning network (PLN)** An online education tool that allows teachers to connect, link, and share resources based on their specific needs.

**Plug-in** A small add-on to existing computer software that allows for increased functionality.

**Podcast** A short recording that can be downloaded from the web onto a mobile device. Although the term 'vodcast' has also surfaced, in this book 'podcast' is used to encompass both audio and video casts.

**Reader** Also known as an 'aggregator'; a program or website that collects content from multiple websites in one place.

**Search engine** A website or app that indexes information on the web, allowing users to find content easily by searching for keywords. See *Keyword*.

**Software as a service** A subscription-based service that allows users to buy software licences on a periodic basis.

**Social network** A website or app that connects users and allows them to share and exchange content about their interests, ideas, experiences, etc.

**Synchronous learning** A teaching method where learning takes place in real time. Contrasts with *Asynchronous learning*.

**Tagging** The process by which a keyword is assigned to a piece of information or a website, allowing users to find the information or website easily the next time they want to access it. See *Keyword*.

**Taxonomy** A system of classifying information into logical categories and sub-categories.

**Toolbar** A strip of buttons used to access the functions of a program, app, or website.

**Upload** The process by which a file is copied from a personal device to the web or a shared network. Contrasts with *Download*.

**Videoconference** Telecommunications software that allows users to communicate in real time.

**Virtual learning environment (VLE)** A software platform with tools and resources that allow teachers and institutions to track, deliver, and report on online learning.

**Virus** A malicious program or piece of code intended to harm your computer.

**Web address** Also known as 'URL'; a unique address used to access a particular website.

**Web browser (browser)** A computer program used to read and display websites.

**WebQuest** A structured, web-based lesson that is centred on using information from the web in relation to higher-order thinking skills, such as comparing, analyzing, and evaluating.

**Widget** A small, stand-alone application that can be embedded into a website and used to perform a specific function (e.g. a clock).

**Wiki** A series of editable web pages created, edited and maintained collaboratively by a community of users.

# Useful websites

### Audio and podcasts

Create and find podcasts and other audio recordings:
http://audacity.sourceforge.net
www.skype.com
www.betteratenglish.com
www.wavosaur.com
www.free-sound-editor.com
https://www.podomatic.com
http://www.podcasts.com
http://www.lyrics.com
www.vocaroo.com

### Blog building websites

Here are some websites to easily create, host, and manage blogs:
www.edublogs.org
https://www.blogger.com
www.wordpress.com

### ELT blogs

Websites by popular ELT educators with lots of good ideas and reflections, and an abundance of links:
www.larryferlazzo.com/english.html
www.nikpeachey.blogspot.com
http://www.vickihollett.com/teaching-blog
https://oupeltglobalblog.com
www.cambridge.org/elt/blog
https://carolread.wordpress.com
www.ddeubel.edublogs.org
https://scottthornbury.wordpress.com

### ELT resources

A collection of useful resources related to ELT:
www.bbc.co.uk/worldservice/learningenglish
www.scoop.it/t/nik-peachey
http://learnenglish.britishcouncil.org/en
www.eslbase.com
www.onestopenglish.com

### Freeware

Free software you can install on your computer, often necessary to run certain types of applications or types of content:

www.adobe.com

www.apple.com

www.winzip.com

### General learning technology resources

Here are some general websites where you can explore innovative ideas around educational technology that go beyond the field of ELT:

www.internet4classrooms.com/esl.htm

www.coolcatteacher.blogspot.com

www.shellyterrell.com

www.freetech4teachers.com

www.call4all.us

www.teach-nology.com

### Image-sharing networks

These websites allow you to post and view collections of photos on the cloud:

www.flickr.com

www.photobucket.com

### Interactive whiteboard

Find here some software for the most popular IWB devices:

https://home.smarttech.com

www.prometheanworld.com

http://mimio.boxlight.com

### Internet safety

Helpful websites for developing computer safety rules for your students and protecting your computer networks:

www.becta.org

www.isafe.org

https://password.kaspersky.com

### Instant engagement systems

https://getkahoot.com

www.socrative.com

### Language e-portfolios

Explore different e-portfolio options here:

www.coe.int/portfolio

www.eelp.org/eportfolio

www.electronicportfolios.org

**Polls and surveys**

Websites for creating polls and surveys that can be used in class, or sent as links:
www.misterpoll.com
www.zoomerang.com
www.surveymonkey.com
www.polleverywhere.com

**Projects**

The following are good places to look for partners to engage in collaborative projects:
www.globalschoolnet.org/gsnpr/index.cfm
https://iearn.org

**Public domain content**

Websites listing resources that are not bound by copyright and are therefore free to use without permission:
www.search.creativecommons.org
https://wikisource.org
www.gutenberg.org
www.archive.org

**Publishing Podcasts**

Use the following resources to upload your own podcasts.
https://soundcloud.com
https://www.blubrry.com
https://www.libsyn.com

**Rubrics**

Use these websites to help you create rules to evaluate student work:
www.etni.org.il/standards/abtrubrics.htm
www.rubistar.4teachers.org
www.edorigami.wikispaces.com

**Social bookmarking**

These websites allow you to save links according to your own criteria:
www.digg.com
http://delicious.com
www.diigo.com

**Social networks**

A list of popular social networks that can be used with your students:
www.facebook.com
www.instagram.com
www.pinterest.com
www.twitter.com
http://eflclassroom.com
www.ning.com
http://eltchat.org/wordpress

### Tutorials

Websites which help explain complex concepts and processes:
www.commoncraft.com
www.teachertrainingvideos.com
www.internet4classrooms.com/on-line.htm
https://support.office.com

### Video

Use these video resources in your classroom. Some websites offer general resources while others are ELT-specific:
www.youtube.com
www.imdb.com/trailers
www.lessonstream.org
www.simpleenglishvideos.com
www.englishcentral.com/videos
www.playposit.com
https://voxy.com

### Video slideshows

A particular genre of video which lets you combine images, audio, and animation into a playable video format:
https://animoto.com
https://studio.stupeflix.com
https://spark.adobe.com
https://flipagram.com

### VLEs

Online education platforms that help you manage learning:
https://moodle.com
www.blackboard.com
www.d2l.com
www.schoology.com
www.canvaslms.com

### WebQuests

Interesting websites with examples of WebQuests and tools for building them:
www.webquest.org
www.zunal.com

### Wikis

Use these collaborative websites for building wikis. These include many additional resources for building learning communities:
www.wikipedia.org
www.pbworks.com
www.wikispaces.com